EYEWITNESS *Travel Guides*

GREEK
PHRASE BOOK

D1303275

DK PUBLISHING, INC.
www.dk.com

489.3
GRE

A DK PUBLISHING BOOK

BT

Compiled by Lexus Ltd with Konstantinos
Kontopidi-Greveniotis and Antigoni Kamberou Miller

First American Edition, 1998
2 4 6 8 10 9 7 5 3 1

Published in the United States by DK Publishing, Inc.
95 Madison Avenue, New York, New York 10016
Visit us on the World Wide Web at www.dk.com

Published in Great Britain by
Dorling Kindersley Limited.

Library of Congress Cataloging-in-Publication Data
Greek phrase book. -- 1st American ed.
     p.   cm. -- (Eyewitness travel guide phrase books)
     ISBN 0–7894–3591–8
     1. Greek language, Modern--Conversation and phrase books--
English.   I. DK Publishing, Inc.   II. Series.
PA1059.G73   1998
489'.383421--DC21   98–7157
                                                     CIP

Picture Credits
Jacket: All special photography Clive Streeter and
Rob Reichenfeld except front cover center right British
Museum/Bridgeman Art Library; front cover top right Peter Wilson.

Printed and bound in Italy by Printer Trento Srl.

CONTENTS

PREFACE

This *Eyewitness Travel Guide Phrase Book* has been compiled by experts to meet the general needs of tourists and business travelers. Arranged under headings such as Hotels, Driving, and so forth, the ample selection of useful words and phrases is supported by a 1,800-line mini-dictionary. There is also an extensive menu guide listing approximately 600 dishes or methods of cooking and presentation.

Typical replies to questions you may ask during your trip, and the signs or instructions you may see or hear, are shown in tinted boxes. In the main text, the pronunciation of Greek words and phrases is imitated in English sound syllables. The Introduction gives basic guidelines to Greek pronunciation.

Eyewitness Travel Guides are recognized as the world's best travel guides. Each title features specially commissioned color photographs, cutaways of major buildings, 3-D aerial views, and detailed maps, plus information on sights, events, hotels, restaurants, shopping, and entertainment.

Eyewitness Travel Guides titles include:
Greece: Athens & the Mainland · The Greek Islands · Amsterdam
Australia · Sydney · California · Florida · Hawaii · New York
San Francisco & Northern California · France · Loire Valley · Paris
Provence · Great Britain · London · Ireland · Istanbul · Italy
Florence & Tuscany · Naples · Rome · Venice & the Veneto
Moscow · St Petersburg · Portugal · Lisbon · Prague · Sardinia
Spain · Seville & Andalusia · Thailand · Vienna · Warsaw

INTRODUCTION

When reading the imitated pronunciation, stress the part that is underlined. Pronounce each syllable as if it formed part of an English word and you will be understood fairly well. Remember the points below and your pronunciation will be even closer to the correct Greek.

e   is always short, as in "bed."

i   is always long, as in "Lolita."

       (So when you see the imitation *ine*, remember to make this two syllables "ee-ne." Similarly, *ne* and *me* should be kept short—*don't* say "nee" or "mee.")

g   should be a rolled, guttural sound at the back of the throat.

h   is a guttural "c," as in "Bach."
       (*Don't* pronounce this as "ck.")

oo   long, as in "moon."

th   as in "then" or "the." Notice this particularly, and *don't* confuse it with TH in small capitals.

TH   as in "theater" or "thin."

On the next page you will find a further guide to Greek pronunciation alongside the Greek alphabet (in both uppercase and lowercase letters).

The Greek Alphabet

To help you read signs or notices printed in uppercase letters (which are sometimes quite unlike their lowercase counterparts), the Greek alphabet is given below. Alongside each letter is its name and a guide to its pronunciation. Until you get used to them, certain letters can be very confusing—for example, the **ro** that looks like an English "P," or the lowercase **ni** that closely resembles an English "v" (and is so similar to the small **ipsilon**).

letter		*name*	*pronunciation*
A	α	alfa	*a* as in "father"
B	β	vita	*v* as in "victory"
Γ	γ	ghamma	before *a, o,* and *u* sounds, it is a guttural *gh* made at the back of the throat; before *e* and *i* sounds, it is like *y* in "yes"
Δ	δ	dhelta	*th* as in "then"
E	ε	epsilon	*e* as in "end"
Z	ζ	zita	*z* as in "zest"
H	η	ita	*i* as in "Maria"
Θ	θ	thita	*th* as in "theater" (TH in the imitated pronunciation system)
I	ι	yiota	before *a* and *o* sounds like *y* in "yes"; otherwise, like *i* in "Maria"
K	κ	kapa	like *k* in "king," but softer
Λ	λ	lamdha	*l* as in "love"
M	μ	mi	*m* as in "mother"
N	ν	ni	*n* as in "no"

Ξ	ξ	ksi	*x* as in "box," or *ks* as in "books"
O	o	omikron	*o* as in "orange"
Π	π	pi	like *p* in "Peter," but softer
P	ρ	ro	*r* as in "Rome," trilled or rolled
Σ	σ,ς	sighma	*s* as in "sing"; the alternative small letter ς is used only at the end of a word
T	τ	taf	like *t* in "tea," but softer
Y	υ	ipsilon	*i* as in "Maria"
Φ	φ	fi	*f* as in "friend"
X	χ	hi	*ch* as in "Bach," but before *e* or *i* sounds, it is like *h* in "hue"
Ψ	ψ	psi	like *ps* in "lapse"
Ω	ω	omegha	*o* as in "orange"

There are several letter combinations that result in totally different sounds. For example, the word for "England" is Αγγλία (or ΑΓΓΛΙΑ in uppercase), and one word for "waiter" is γκαρσόνι or γκαρσόν: the combination γκ produces a hard "g" as in "go," while γγ makes an "ng" as in "England."

Another combination that results in a new sound is ντ: most of the time this begins with a slight "n" sound (like the "nd" in "bind"), but at the beginning of a word it is like the "d" in "dog" unless the previous word ends in a vowel. Don't worry about this—use either, but keep the "n" ineffectual. Finally, the combination μπ is pronounced like the English "b."

Note that the Greek question mark is a semicolon. Stress is indicated by an accent above the Greek letter and an underline in the pronuciation.

USEFUL EVERYDAY PHRASES

Yes/No
Ναι/Όχι
ne/ohi

Thank you
Ευχαριστώ
efharisto

No, thank you
Όχι, ευχαριστώ
ohi efharisto

Please
Παρακαλώ
parakalo

I don't understand
Δεν καταλαβαίνω
then katalaveno

Do you speak English/French/German?
Μιλάτε Αγγλικά/Γαλλικά/Γερμανικά;
milate Anglika/Galika/Yermanika

I can't speak Greek
Δέν μιλάω Ελληνικά
then milao elinika

Please speak more slowly
Παρακαλώ, μιλάτε πιό αργά;
parakalo, milate pio arga

Please write it down for me
Μου το γράφετε, παρακαλώ;
moo to grafete, parakalo

Good morning/good afternoon/good night
Καλημέρα/καλησπέρα/καληνύχτα
kalimera/kalispera/kalinihta

Good-bye
Αντίο
andio

How are you?
Τι κάνεις;
ti kanis

Excuse me, please
Συγγνώμη, παρακαλώ
singnomi, parakalo

Sorry!
Συγγνώμη!
singnomi

I'm really sorry
Ειλικρινά, λυπάμαι
ilikrina, lipame

Can you help me?
Μπορείς να με βοηθήσεις;
boris na me voiTHisis

Can you tell me . . . ?
Μου λέτε . . . ;
moo lete

Can I have . . . ?
Μπορώ να έχω . . . ;
boro̱ na e̱ho

I would like . . .
Θα ήθελα . . .
тнa i̱тнela

Is there . . . here?
Υπάρχει . . . εδώ;
ipa̱rhi . . . etho̱

Where are the restrooms?
Που είναι οι τουαλέτες;
poo i̱ne i tooale̱tes

Where can I get . . . ?
Που μπορώ να πάρω . . . ;
poo boro̱ na pa̱ro

How much is it?
Πόσο κάνει;
po̱so ka̱ni

Do you take credit cards?
Δέχεστε πιστωτικές κάρτες;
the̱heste pistotike̱s ka̱rtes

Can I pay by check?
Μπορώ να πληρώσω με επιταγή;
boro̱ na pliro̱so me epitayi̱

What time is it?
Τι ώρα είναι;
ti o̱ra i̱ne

I must go now
Πρέπει να πηγαίνω τώρα
prepi na piyeno tora

Cheers! *(toast)*
Εις υγείαν!
is iyian

Go away!
Παράτα με!
paratame

THINGS YOU'LL SEE OR HEAR

ανακοίνωση	*anakinosi*	announcement
ΑΝΑΧΩΡΗΣΕΙΣ/	*anahorisis*	departures
αναχωρήσεις		
ΑΝΟΙΚΤΑ/ανοικτά	*anikta*	open
ΑΝΟΙΚΤΟΝ/ανοικτόν	*anikton*	open
ΑΣΑΝΣΕΡ/ασανσέρ	*asanser*	elevator
αντίο	*andio*	good-bye
απαγορεύεται	*apagorevete*	no smoking
το κάπνισμα	*to kapnisma*	
αργά	*arga*	slow
αριστερά	*aristera*	left
ΑΦΙΞΕΙΣ/αφίξεις	*afixis*	arrivals
βιβλιοθήκη	*vivlioTHiki*	library
ΓΥΝΑΙΚΩΝ/γυναικών	*yinekon*	women's restroom
ΔΕΝ ΛΕΙΤΟΥΡΓΕΙ/	*then litooryi*	out of order
δεν λειτουργεί		
δεξιά	*thexia*	right
διάλειμμα	*thialima*	interval
ΕΙΣΟΔΟΣ/είσοδος	*isothos*	entrance
έκθεση	*ekTHesi*	exhibition, show room

→

11

έλεγχος	elenhos	check, inspection
ελεύθερος	elefTHeros	free
ΕΞΟΔΟΣ/έξοδος	exothos	exit
ευχαριστώ	efharisto	thank you
καλώς ήρθατε	kalos irtHate	welcome
ΚΑΠΝΙΖΟΝΤΕΣ/ καπνίζοντες	kapnizodes	smokers
ΚΑΤΗΛΗΜΜΕΝΟΣ/ κατηλημμένος	katilimenos	occupied
ΚΙΝΔΥΝΟΣ/κίνδυνος	kinthinos	danger
ΚΛΕΙΣΤΑ/κλειστά	klista	closed
ΚΛΕΙΣΤΟΝ/κλειστόν	kliston	closed
μέχρι	mehri	until
μη	mi	do not
ναί	ne	yes
ορίστε;	oriste?	can I help you?
όχι	ohi	no
παρακαλώ	parakalo	please; can I help you?
πεζοί	pezi	pedestrians
προσοχή παρακαλώ	prosohi parakalo	attention, please
ΠΡΟΣΟΧΗ!/προσοχή!	prosohi	caution!
ΣΥΡΑΤΕ/σύρατε	sirate	pull
ΣΤΟΠ/στόπ	stop	stop
στρίψατε	stripsate	turn
ΣΧΟΛΕΙΟ/σχολείο	s-holio	school
ΤΑΜΕΙΟ/ταμείο	tamio	cash register
ΤΕΛΩΝΕΙΟ/Τελωνείο	Telonio	customs
ΤΟΥΡΙΣΤΙΚΗ ΑΣΤΥΝΟΜΙΑ/ Τουριστική Αστυνομία	Tooristiki Astinomia	Tourist Police
χαίρετε	herete	hello
ωθήσατε	oTHisate	push
ώρες λειτουργίας	ores litooryias	opening hours

DAYS, MONTHS, SEASONS

Sunday	η Κυριακή	i kiriaki
Monday	η Δευτέρα	i theftera
Tuesday	η Τρίτη	i triti
Wednesday	η Τετάρτη	i tetarti
Thursday	η Πέμπτη	i pembti
Friday	η Παρασκευή	i paraskevi
Saturday	το Σάββατο	to savato
January	Ιανουάριος	ianooarios
February	Φεβρουάριος	fevrooarios
March	Μάρτιος	martios
April	Απρίλιος	aprilios
May	Μάιος	maios
June	Ιούνιος	ioonios
July	Ιούλιος	ioolios
August	Αύγουστος	avgoostos
September	Σεπτέμβριος	septemvrios
October	Οκτώβριος	oktovrios
November	Νοέμβριος	noemvrios
December	Δεκέμβριος	thekemvrios
Spring	η άνοιξη	i anixi
Summer	το καλοκαίρι	to kalokeri
Autumn	το φθινόπωρο	to fτHinoporo
Winter	ο χειμώνας	o himonas
Christmas	τα Χριστούγεννα	ta hristooyena
Christmas Eve	η παραμονή Χριστουγέννων	i paramoni hristooyenon
Good Friday	η Μεγάλη Παρασκευή	i megali paraskevi
Easter	το Πάσχα	to pas-ha
New Year	η Πρωτοχρονιά	i protohronia
New Year's Eve	η Παραμονή Πρωτοχρονιάς	i paramoni protohronias

NUMBERS

0 μηδέν *mithen*
1 ένα *ena*
2 δύο *thio*
3 τρία *tria*
4 τέσσερα *tesera*

5 πέντε *pende*
6 έξι *exi*
7 επτά *epta*
8 οχτώ *ohto*
9 εννιά *enia*

10 δέκα *theka*
11 έντεκα *edeka*
12 δώδεκα *thotheka*
13 δεκατρία *theka-tria*
14 δεκατέσσερα *theka-tesera*
15 δεκαπέντε *theka-pende*
16 δεκαέξι *theka-exi*
17 δεκαεπτά *theka-epta*
18 δεκαοκτώ *theka-ohto*
19 δεκαεννιά *theka-enia*
20 είκοσι *ikosi*
21 εικοσιένα *ikosi-ena*
22 εικοσιδύο *ikosi-thio*
30 τριάντα *trianda*
31 τριανταένα *trianda-ena*
32 τριανταδύο *trianda-thio*
40 σαράντα *saranda*
50 πενήντα *peninda*
60 εξήντα *exinda*
70 εβδομήντα *evthomida*
80 ογδόντα *ogthonda*
90 ενενήντα *eneninda*
100 εκατό *ekato*
110 εκατόν δέκα *ekaton theka*
200 διακόσια *thiakosia*
1000 χίλια *hilia*
1,000,000 ένα εκατομμύριο *ena ekatomirio*

14

TIME

today	σήμερα	simera
yesterday	χτες	htes
tomorrow	αύριο	avrio
the day before yesterday	προχτές	prohtes
the day after tomorrow	μεθαύριο	meTHavrio
this week	αυτή την εβδομάδα	afti tin evthomatha
last week	την περασμένη εβδομάδα	tin perasmeni evthomatha
next week	την επόμενη εβδομάδα	tin epomeni evthomatha
this morning	το πρωί	to proi
this afternoon	το απόγευμα	to apoyevma
this evening	το βράδυ	to vrathi
tonight	απόψε	apopse
yesterday afternoon	χτες το απόγευμα	htes t'apoyevma
last night	χτες τη νύχτα	htes ti nihta
tomorrow morning	αύριο το πρωί	avrio to proi
tomorrow night	αύριο το βράδυ	avrio to vrathi
in three days	σε τρεις μέρες	se tris meres
three days ago	πριν τρεις μέρες	prin tris meres
late	αργά	arga
early	νωρίς	noris
soon	σύντομα	sindoma
later on	αργότερα	argotera
at the moment	προς το παρόν	pros to paron
second	το δευτερόλεπτο	to thefterolepto
minute	το λεπτό	to lepto
ten minutes	δέκα λεπτά	theka lepta
quarter of an hour	ένα τέταρτο	ena tetarto
half an hour	μισή ώρα	misi ora

three quarters of an hour	τρία τέταρτα της ώρας	tria tetarta tis oras
hour	η ώρα	i ora
day	η μέρα	i mera
week	η εβδομάδα	i evthomatha
two weeks	σε δύο εβδομάδες	se thio evthomathes
month	ο μήνας	o minas
year	ο χρόνος	o hronos

TELLING TIME

In Greek you always put the hour first and then use the word ke (και) to denote the minutes "past" the hour and **para** (παρά) for the minutes "to" the hour (e.g., "five-twenty" = **5 ke 20**; "five-forty" = **6 para 20**). The 24-hour clock is used officially in timetables and inquiry offices. Don't forget that Greek Standard Time is always seven hours ahead of Eastern Standard Time.

one o'clock	μία η ώρα	mia i ora
ten past one	μία και δέκα	mia ke theka
quarter past one	μία και τέταρτο	mia ke tetarto
twenty past one	μία και είκοσι	mia ke ikosi
1:30	μία και μισή	mia ke misi
twenty to two	δύο παρά είκοσι	thio para ikosi
quarter to two	δύο παρά τέταρτο	thio para tetarto
ten to two	δύο παρά δέκα	thio para theka
two o'clock	δύο η ώρα	thio i ora
13:00 (1 PM)	δεκατρείς	theka-tris
16:30 (4:30 PM)	δεκαέξι και τριάντα	theka-exi ke trianda
20:10 (8:10 PM)	είκοσι και δέκα	ikosi ke theka
at 5:30	στις πέντε και μισή	stis pede ke misi
at seven o'clock	στις επτά	stis epta
noon	το μεσημέρι	to mesimeri
midnight	τα μεσάνυχτα	ta mesanihta

HOTELS

Depending on the visitor's preferences and on what they are prepared to spend, there is a choice of hotels, apartment hotels, self-catering accommodations, and rooms in private houses.

Hotels are divided into six categories: De Luxe or AA, and 1st to 5th Class or A to E. In most hotels a 15 percent service charge is added to your bill. For information about hotels, contact the Greek National Tourist Organization, 645 Fifth Avenue, New York, New York 10022. If you are traveling in the more popular areas during peak season it is always advisable to book accommodations in advance.

USEFUL WORDS AND PHRASES

balcony	το μπαλκόνι	to balk<u>o</u>ni
bathroom	το λουτρό	to lootr<u>o</u>
bed	το κρεβάτι	to krev<u>a</u>ti
bedroom	το υπνοδωμάτιο	to ipnothom<u>a</u>tio
bill	ο λογαριασμός	o logariasm<u>o</u>s
breakfast	το πρωινό	to proin<u>o</u>
dining room	η τραπεζαρία	i trapezar<u>i</u>a
dinner	το δείπνο	to th<u>i</u>pno
double room	το διπλό δωμάτιο	to thipl<u>o</u> thom<u>a</u>tio
elevator	το ασανσέρ	to asans<u>e</u>r
foyer	το φουαγέ	to fooay<u>e</u>
full board	η φουλ-πανσιόν	i fool-pansi<u>o</u>n
half board	η ντεμί-πανσιόν	i dem<u>i</u>-pansi<u>o</u>n
hotel	το ξενοδοχείο	to xenothoh<u>i</u>o
key	το κλειδί	to klith<u>i</u>
lounge	το σαλόνι	to sal<u>o</u>ni
lunch	το γεύμα	to y<u>e</u>vma
manager	ο διευθυντής	o thi-efTHind<u>i</u>s
receipt	η απόδειξη	i ap<u>o</u>thixi
reception	η ρεσεψιόν	i resepsi<u>o</u>n

receptionist	ο ρεσεψιονίστας	o resepsionistas
restaurant	το εστιατόριο	to estiatorio
restroom	η τουαλέτα	i tooaleta
room	το δωμάτιο	to thomatio
room service	το σέρβις δωματίου	to servis thomatioo
shower	το ντους	to doos
single room	το μονό δωμάτιο	to mono thomatio
twin room	το δωμάτιο με	to thomatio me
	δύο κρεβάτια	thio krevatia

Do you have any vacancies?
Εχετε κενά δωμάτια;
ehete kena thomatia

I have a reservation
Εχω κλείσει δωμάτιο
eho klisi thomatio

I'd like a single room
Θα ήθελα ένα μονό δωμάτιο
THa ithela ena mono thomatio

I'd like a double room
Θα ήθελα ένα δωμάτιο με διπλό κρεβάτι
THa ithela ena thomatio me thiplo krevati

I'd like a twin room
Θα ήθελα ένα δωμάτιο με δύο κρεβάτια
THa ithela ena thomatio me thio krevatia

I'd like a room with a bathroom/balcony
Θα ήθελα ένα δωμάτιο με μπάνιο/μπαλκόνι
THa ithela ena thomatio me banio/balkoni

I'd like a room for one night/three nights
Θα ήθελα ένα δωμάτιο για μία νύχτα/τρεις νύχτες
THα i̱THela e̱na thoma̱tio ya mi̱a ni̱hta/tris ni̱htes

What is the charge per night?
Πόσο στοιχίζει η διανυκτέρευση;
po̱so stihi̱zi i thianihte̱refsi

THINGS YOU'LL HEAR

Then iparhoon mona/thipla thomatia kena
There are no single/double rooms left

Imaste yemati
No vacancies

Parakalo, plironete prokatavolika?
Please pay in advance

Parakalo, afinete to thiavatsrio sas etho?
Please leave your passport here

I don't know yet how long I'll stay
Δεν ξέρω ακόμα πόσο καιρό θα μείνω
then xe̱ro ako̱ma po̱so kero̱ THα mi̱no

When is breakfast/dinner?
Πότε έχει πρωινό/δείπνο;
po̱te e̱hi proino̱/thi̱pno

Would you have my baggage brought up?
Θα μου φέρετε τις βαλίτσες μου;
THα moo fe̱rete tis vali̱tses moo

Please call me at . . . o'clock
Παρακαλώ ειδοποιήστε με στις . . .
parakalo ithopi-isteme stis

May I have breakfast in my room?
Μπορώ να πάρω το πρωινό στο δωμάτιό μου;
boro na paro to proino sto thomatio moo

I'll be back at . . . o'clock
Θα επιστρέψω στις . . .
THa epistrepso stis

My room number is . . .
Ο αριθμός του δωματιού μου είναι . . .
o ariTHmos too thomatioo moo ine

I'm leaving tomorrow
Φεύγω αύριο
fevgo avrio

May I have the bill, please?
Τον λογαριασμό παρακαλώ
ton logariasmo parakalo

Can you get me a taxi?
Μου καλείτε ένα ταξί;
moo kalite ena taxi

Can you recommend another hotel?
Μπορείτε να μου προτείνετε κάποιο άλλο ξενοδοχείο;
borite na moo protinete kapio alo xenothohio

THINGS YOU'LL SEE

ασανσέρ	*asanser*	elevator
γκαράζ	*garaz*	garage
δείπνο	*thipno*	dinner
διπλό δωμάτιο	*thiplo thomatio*	double room
δωμάτια	*thomatia*	rooms
είσοδος	*isothos*	entrance
ενοικιάζονται δωμάτια	*enikianzode thomatia*	rooms to rent
ΕΟΤ		Greek National Tourist Organization
έξοδος κινδύνου	*exothos kinthinoo*	emergency exit
εστιατόριο	*estiatorio*	restaurant
ισόγειο	*isoyio*	ground floor
λογαριασμός	*logariasmos*	bill
λουτρό	*lootro*	bathroom
μονό δωμάτιο	*mono thomatio*	single room
ντους	*doos*	shower
ξενοδοχείο	*xenothohio*	hotel
πλήρες	*plires*	full, no vacancies
πρωινό	*proino*	breakfast
πρώτος όροφος	*protos orofos*	second floor
ρεσεψιόν	*resepsion*	reception
σκάλες	*skales*	stairs
σύρατε	*sirate*	pull
τουαλέτες	*tooaletes*	restrooms
υπόγειο	*ipoyio*	basement
φαγητό	*fayito*	meal, lunch
ωθήσατε	*oTHisate*	push

CAMPING AND TRAILER TRAVEL

There are plenty of organized camping sites run by EOT (the Greek National Tourist Organization) and these are often situated in some of the most picturesque parts of the country. Campsites are usually open from March to November. In addition to the state-run campsites, there are also a large number of sites run by licensed private individuals. Further details about these camping sites can be supplied by EOT information offices in Greece or in Los Angeles, Chicago, or New York City, as well as by the Greek Tourist Police, who have an office in every major Greek town. If you are camping in Greece you should remember that it is forbidden to camp anywhere other than in a proper site.

Youth hostels are open to members of the YHA (Youth Hostels Association). Stays are limited to ten nights.

Useful Words and Phrases

backpack	το σακίδιο	*to sakithio*
bucket	ο κουβάς	*o koovas*
camper	το τροχόσπιτο	*to trohospito*
camper site	το κάμπινγκ για τροχόσπιτα	*to "camping" ya trohospita*
campfire	φωτιά	*fotia*
go camping	κατασκηνώνω	*kataskinono*
campsite	το κάμπινγκ	*to "camping"*
cooking utensils	τα σκεύη μαγειρικής	*ta skevi mayirikis*
drinking water	το πόσιμο νερό	*to posimo nero*
garbage	τα σκουπίδια	*ta skoopithia*
ground cloth	ο μουσαμάς	*o moosamas*
hitchhike	κάνω ωτο-στόπ	*kano oto-stop*
rope	το σχοινί	*to s-hini*
saucepans	τα κατσαρολικά	*ta katsarolika*

sleeping bag	το σλίπινγκ μπαγκ	*to "sleeping bag"*
tent	η σκηνή	*i skini*
youth hostel	ο ξενώνας νέων	*o xenonas neon*

Can I camp here?
Μπορώ να κατασκηνώσω εδώ;
boro na kataskinoso etho

Can we park the camper here?
Μπορούμε να παρκάρουμε το τροχόσπιτο εδώ;
boroome na parkaroome to trohospito etho

Where is the nearest campsite?
Που είναι το πλησιέστερο κάμπινγκ;
poo ine to plisi-estero 'camping'

What is the charge per night?
Πόσο στοιχίζει η διανυκτέρευση;
poso stihizi i thianikterefsi

What facilities are there?
Τι ευκολίες υπάρχουν εκεί;
ti efkoli-es iparhoon eki

Can I light a fire here?
Μπορώ ν' ανάψω φωτιά εδώ;
boro n' anapso fotia etho

Where can I get . . . ?
Που μπορώ να βρώ . . . ;
poo boro na vro

Is there drinking water here?
Υπάρχει πόσιμο νερό εδώ;
iparhi posimo nero etho

THINGS YOU'LL SEE

απαγορεύεται	*apagorevete*	no camping
το κάμπινγκ	*to "camping"*	
κάμπινγκ	*"camping"*	campsite
κουβέρτα	*kooverta*	blanket
κουζίνα	*koozina*	kitchen
νερό	*nero*	water
ντους	*doos*	shower
ξενώνας νέων	*xenonas neon*	youth hostel
πόσιμο νερό	*posimo nero*	drinking water
ριμουλκό	*rimoolko*	trailer
σκηνή	*skini*	tent
σλίπινγκ μπαγκ	*"sleeping bag"*	sleeping bag
ταυτότητα	*taftotita*	pass, identity card
τιμή	*timi*	charges
τουαλέτες	*tooualetes*	restrooms
τροχόσπιτα	*trohospita*	campers
φως	*fos*	light
φωτιά	*fotia*	fire
χρησιμοποιείται . . .	*hrisimopi-ite . . .*	use . . .

DRIVING

Most roads in Greece are single-lane only. It is best to use the national highways (*eTHniki*), since they often have separate lanes for slow, heavy vehicles, which makes passing much easier. They join Patra with Athens if you are coming by ferry from Italy, and the Greek-Macedonian border with Thessaloniki and Athens if you are coming into Greece through Austria and the former Yugoslavia. Secondary roads are not so good and can often be in quite poor condition. Holders of US driver's licenses do not need an international driver's license.

The Greek Automobile and Touring Club (ELPA) offers assistance to foreign motorists free of charge if they are members of an automobile club. When renting a car or a motorcycle you might find that your passport will be kept until you return. Motorcycles can be rented without a license.

The rules of the road are: drive on the right, pass on the left. Priority at intersections is as indicated by standard international signs. At intersections without road signs, vehicles coming from the right have priority. The speed limit on the national highways is 110 km/h (68 mph); at other times, keep to the speed shown. In built-up areas the limit is 50 km/h (31 mph).

There are plenty of service stations around the main towns. Gas stations on the highways are usually open 24 hours a day, but elsewhere they close early at night. Fuel ratings are as follows: "Super" should be used by all modern cars, "Regular" should be used for small motorcycles only. Greek gas is the most expensive in Europe. Diesel fuel is about half the price of gas.

SOME COMMON ROAD SIGNS

αδιέξοδο	*athiexotho*	dead end
απαγορεύεται η στάθμευση	*apagorevete i staTHmefsi*	no parking
γραμμές τραίνου	*grames trenoo*	railroad crosses road
διάβαση πεζών	*thiavasi pezon*	pedestrian crossing
διόδια	*thiothia*	toll
έξοδος αυτοκινήτων	*exothos aftokiniton*	vehicle exit
έργα	*erga*	road work
ιδιωτικός δρόμος	*ithiotikos thromos*	private road
ισόπεδος διάβασις	*isopethos thiavasis*	railroad crossing
κάμπινγκ	*"camping"*	campsite
κέντρο	*kendro*	center
κίνδυνος πυρκαγιάς	*kinthinos pirkayas*	fire risk
μονόδρομος	*monothromos*	one-way street
νομός	*nomos*	county
οδός	*othos*	street, road
παραλία	*paralia*	beach
πεζοί	*pezi*	pedestrians
πρατήριο βενζίνης	*pratirio venzinis*	gas station
προσοχή	*prosohi*	caution
στοπ	*"stop"*	stop
σχολείο	*s-holio*	school
τέλος	*telos*	end
τροχαία	*trohea*	traffic police
χιλιόμετρα	*hiliometra*	kilometers

Useful Words and Phrases

brake	το φρένο	to freno
breakdown	η μηχανική βλάβη	i mihaniki vlavi
camper	το τροχόσπιτο	to trohospito
car	το αυτοκίνητο	to aftokinito
drive (verb)	οδηγώ	othigo
engine	η μηχανή	i mihani
exhaust	η εξάτμηση	i exatmisi
fan belt	το λουρί του βεντιλατέρ	to loori too ventilater
garage (for repairs)	το συνεργείο	to sineryio
gas	η βενζίνη	i venzini
gas station	το βενζινάδικο	to venzinathiko
gear	η ταχύτητα	i tahitita
gears	οι ταχύτητες	i tahitites
headlights	τα μπροστινά φώτα	ta brostina fota
highway	η εθνική οδός	i ethniki othos
hood	το καπό	to kapo
intersection	η διασταύρωση	i thiastavrosi
junction (on highway)	η έξοδος	i exothos
license	το δίπλωμα οδηγού	to thiploma othiyoo
license plate	οι πινακίδες	i pinakithes
mirror	ο καθρέφτης	o kathreftis
motorcycle	το μηχανάκι	to mihanaki
road	ο δρόμος	o thromos
skid (verb)	γλυστράω	glistrao
spare parts	τα ανταλακτικά	ta andalaktika
speed	η ταχύτητα	i tahitita
speed limit	το όριο ταχύτητας	to orio tahititas
speedometer	το κοντέρ	to konter
steering wheel	το τιμόνι	to timoni
taillights	τα πίσω φώτα	ta piso fota
tire	το λάστιχο	to lastiho
tow (verb)	τραβάω	travao

traffic lights	τα φανάρια	*ta fanaria*
trailer	το ριμουλκό	*to rimoolko*
truck	το φορτηγό	*to fortigo*
trunk	το πορτ-μπαγκάζ	*to port-bagaz*
van	το φορτηγάκι	*to fortigaki*
wheel	η ρόδα	*i rotha*
windshield	το παρμπρίζ	*to parbriz*

I'd like some gas
Θέλω βενζίνη
THelo venzini

I'd like some oil/water
Θέλω λάδι/νερό
THelo lathi/nero

Fill her up, please
Το γεμίζετε παρακαλώ;
to yemizete, parakalo

I'd like 10 liters of gas
Θέλω δέκα λίτρα βενζίνη
THelo theka litra venzini

How do I get to . . . ?
Πως μπορώ να πάω . . . ;
pos boro na pao

Is this the road to . . . ?
Αυτός είναι ο δρόμος για . . . ;
aftos ine o thromos ya

Where is the nearest gas station?
Πού είναι το πλησιέστερο βενζινάδικο;
poo ine to plisi-estero venzinathiko

DIRECTIONS YOU MAY BE GIVEN

efτΗia	straight ahead
pernas to/ti . . .	go past the . . .
staristera	on the left
sta thexia	on the right
stripse aristera	turn left
stripse thexia	turn right
theftero aristera	second on the left
to proto thexia	first on the right

Would you check the tires, please?
Ελέγχετε τα λάστιχα, παρακαλώ;
elenhete ta lastiha, parakalo

Do you do repairs?
Κάνετε επισκευές;
kanete episkeves

Can you repair the clutch?
Μου φτιάχνετε το ντεμπραγιάζ;
moo ftighnete to debrayaz

How long will it take?
Πόσο θα κάνει;
poso τΗa kani

There is something wrong with the engine
Κάτι δεν πάει καλά με τη μηχανή
kati then pai kala me ti mihani

The engine is overheating
Η μηχανή υπερθερμαίνεται
i mihani iperτΗermenete

The brakes are binding
Τα φρένα κολλάνε
ta frena kolane

I need a new tire
Χρειάζομαι καινούργιο λάστιχο
hriazome kenooryio lastiho

Where can I park?
Που μπορώ να παρκάρω;
poo boro na parkaro

Can I park here?
Μπορώ να παρκάρω εδώ;
boro na parkaro etho

I'd like to rent a car
Θέλω να νοικιάσω ένα αυτοκίνητο
THelo na nikiaso ena aftokinito

THINGS YOU'LL SEE

αεραντλία	*aerandlia*	air pump
αλλαγή λαδιών	*alayi lathion*	oil change
ανοικτόν	*anikton*	open
ανταλλακτικά αυτοκινήτων	*andalaktika aftokiniton*	spare parts
αντιπροσωπεία αυτοκινήτων	*andiprosopia aftokiniton*	car dealer
αντλία βενζίνης	*andlia venzinis*	gas pump
απλή	*apli*	regular
αστυνομία	*astinomia*	police
βαφές αυτοκινήτων	*vafes aftokiniton*	auto-body shop
βενζίνη	*venzini*	gas
βουλκανιζατέρ	*voolkanizater*	tire repairs
γκαράζ	*garaz*	parking garage
εθνική οδός	*eTHniki othos*	highway
ελαστικά	*elastika*	tires
ενοικιάζονται αυτοκίνητα	*enikiazonde aftokinita*	car rental
εξατμίσεις	*exatmisis*	exhausts
έξοδος	*exothos*	exit
ηλεκτρολόγος αυτοκινήτων	*ilektrologos aftokiniton*	car electrician
λάδια	*lathia*	engine oil
σβήστε τη μηχανή	*sviste ti mihani*	turn off engine
σούπερ	*"super"*	4-star gas
συνεργείο	*sineryio*	car repairs

TRAIN AND BOAT TRAVEL

Hellenic Railroads Organization (ΟΣΕ) operates the country's railroad network. The trains are modern and there is regular and comfortable service to the most important regions of the mainland. The network is otherwise not very extensive. There are first and second class season tickets at reduced rates that permit the holders to travel as many times as they wish. Trains are inexpensive—a round-trip ticket costs 20 percent less than two one-way tickets. Children 14 or under travel at half price.

Boats connect the mainland with all the major islands, and there are frequent ferries to most islands from Piraeus. Altogether there are about 200 ports in the Greek islands and 50 ports on the mainland. The islands are interconnected by sea routes and, for excursions, there are daily around-the-island trips or visits to other nearby islands.

USEFUL WORDS AND PHRASES

baggage cart	το καροτσάκι	to karotsáki
baggage room	ο χώρος φύλαξης αποσκευών	o horos filaxis aposkevon
boat	το πλοίο	to plio
buffet	το μπαρ	to bar
car ferry	το φέρρυ-μπωτ	to feri-bot
carriage	το βαγόνι	to vagoni
connection	η σύνδεση	i sinthesi
currency exchange	το συνάλλαγμα	to sinalagma
dining car	η τραπεζαρία του τραίνου	trapezaria too trenoo
docks	η προκυμαία	i prokimea
engine	η μηχανή	i mihani
entrance	η είσοδος	i isothos
exit	η έξοδος	i exothos
ferry	το φέρρυ-μπωτ	to feri-bot
first class	η πρώτη θέση	i proti THEsi

get in	μπαίνω	beno
get out	βγαίνω	v-yeno
lost and found	τα απολεσθέντα αντικείμενα	ta apoles-THenda andikimena
platform	η πλατφόρμα	i platforma
port	το λιμάνι	to limani
rail	οι γραμμές	i grames
railroad	ο σιδηρόδρομος	o sithirothromos
reservation office	το πρακτορείο	to praktorio
reserved seat	η κλεισμένη θέση	i klismeni THesi
restaurant car	το βαγόνι εστιατορίου	to vagoni estiatorioo
round-trip ticket	το εισιτήριο μετ'επιστροφής	to isitirio metepistrofis
sea	η θάλασσα	i THalasa
seat	η θέση	i THesi
ship	το πλοίο	to plio
station	ο σταθμός	o staTHmos
station master	ο σταθμάρχης	o staTHmarhis
ticket	το εισιτήριο	to isitirio
ticket collector	ο εισπράκτορας	o ispraktoras
timetable	τα δρομολόγια	ta thromoloyia
train	το τραίνο	to treno
waiting room	η αίθουσα αναμονής	i eTHoosa anamonis
window	το παράθυρο	to paraTHiro

When does the boat for . . . leave?
Πότε φεύγει το πλοίο για . . . ;
pote fev-yi to plio ya

When does the train from . . . arrive?
Πότε έρχεται το τραίνο από . . . ;
pote erhete to treno apo

When is the next/first/last boat to . . . ?
Πότε είναι το επόμενο/πρώτο/τελευταίο πλοίο για . . . ;
pote ine to epomeno/proto/telefteo plio ya

What is the fare to . . . ?
Πόσο κάνει το εισιτήριο για . . . ;
poso kani to isitirio ya

Do I have to change?
Πρέπει ν'αλλάξω;
prepi nalaxo

Does the boat/train stop at . . . ?
Σταματάει στη . . . ;
stamatai sti

How long does it take to get to . . . ?
Πόσες ώρες κάνει να φθάσει . . . ;
poses ores kani na ftHasi

A one-way/round-trip ticket to . . . , please
Ένα απλό/μετ'επιστροφής εισιτήριο για . . . παρακαλώ
ena aplo/metepistrofis isitirio ya . . . parakalo

I'd like to reserve a seat
Θέλω να κλείσω μία θέση
THelo na kliso mia THesi

Is this the right boat for . . . ?
Αυτό είναι το πλοίο για . . . ;
afto ine to plio ya

Is there a car ferry to . . . ?
Υπάρχει φέρρυ-μπωτ για . . . ;
iparhi feri-bot ya

Is this the right platform for the . . . train?
Αυτή είναι η σωστή πλατφόρμα γιά το τραίνο προς . . . ;
afti ine i sosti platforma ya to treno pros

Which platform for the . . . train?
Σε ποιά πλατφόρμα γιά το τραίνο προς . . . ;
se pia platforma ya to treno pros

Is the boat late?
Έχει καθυστέρηση το πλοίο;
ehi kaTHisterisi to plio

Could you help me with my baggage, please?
Μπορείτε να με βοηθήσετε με τις αποσκευές μου,
   παρακαλώ;
borite na me voiTHisete me tis aposkeves moo, parakalo

Is this a nonsmoking compartment?
Είναι για τους μη καπνίζοντες;
ine ya toos mi kapnizondes

Is this seat free?
Είναι ελεύθερη αυτή η θέση;
ine elefTHeri afti i THesi

This seat is taken
Αυτή η θέση είναι πιασμένη
afti i THesi ine piasmeni

I have reserved this seat
Έχω κλείσει αυτή τη θέση
eho klisi afti ti THesi

May I open/close the window?
Μπορώ ν'ανοίξω/κλείσω το παράθυρο;
boro nanixo/kliso to paraTHiro

When do we arrive in . . . ?
Πότε φτάνουμε στο . . . ;
pote ftanoome sto

Which island is this?
Ποιό νησί είναι αυτό;
pio nisi ine afto

Do we stop at . . . ?
Σταματάμε στο . . . ;
stamatame sto

Would you keep an eye on my things for a moment?
Μπορείτε να προσέξετε τα πράγματά μου για ένα λεπτό;
borite na prosexete ta pragmata moo ya ena lepto

Is there a restaurant car on this train?
Υπάρχει βαγόνι εστιατορίου σ'αυτό το τραίνο;
iparhi vagoni estiatorioo safto to treno

THINGS YOU'LL SEE

ακριβές αντίτιμο μόνο	*akriv_es and_itimo m_ono*	exact fare only
ακτή	*akt_i*	beach
αριθμός θέσεως	*ariTHm_os TH_eseos*	seat number
αφετηρία	*afetir_ia*	terminal
διαβατήρια	*thiavat_iria*	passports
δρομολόγια	*thromol_oyia*	timetable
εισιτήρια	*isit_iria*	tickets
καμπίνες	*kab_ines*	cabins
καπετάνιος	*kapet_anios*	captain
κατάστρωμα	*kat_astroma*	deck
λέμβος	*l_emvos*	lifeboat
λιμενάρχης	*limen_arhis*	harbor master
λιμήν	*lim_in*	port, harbor
λογιστήριο	*loyist_irio*	purser's office
Ο/Γ		ferry
ΟΣΕ	*os_e*	Hellenic Railroads Organization
προς γκαράζ	*pros gar_az*	to car deck
σωσίβια	*sos_ivia*	life preservers
τουαλέτες	*tooal_etes*	restrooms
τραπεζαρία	*trapezar_ia*	dining room (boat)

AIR TRAVEL

Air services connect Greece with all the major airports of the world. Olympic Airways and many other international and US airlines provide services between major cities in the US and the following Greek destinations: Athens, Thessaloniki, and the islands of Corfu, Rhodes, Crete, and Mykonos. There is also an extensive domestic network run by Olympic Airways (OA) connecting the main towns, islands, and tourist centers. In Athens the Eastern terminal of the airport serves all foreign airlines, and the Western terminal caters to all domestic and international OA flights.

USEFUL WORDS AND PHRASES

aircraft	το αεροπλάνο	to aeroplano
airline	οι αερογραμμές	i aerogrames
airport	το αεροδρόμιο	to aerothromio
airport shuttle	το λεωφορείο του αεροδρομίου	to leoforio too aerothromioo
aisle seat	η θέση δίπλα στο διάδρομο	i THesi thipla sto thiathromo
baggage claim	οι αεροσκευές	i aposkeves
boarding pass	η κάρτα αναχώρησης	i karta anahorisis
check-in (noun)	το τσεκ-ιν	to "check-in"
delay	η καθυστέρηση	i kaTHisterisi
departure	η αναχώρηση	i anahorisi
departure lounge	η αίθουσα αναχωρήσεων	i eTHoosa anahoriseon
emergency exit	η έξοδος κινδύνου	i exothos kinthinoo
flight	η πτήση	i ptisi
flight attendant		
(female)	η αεροσυνοδός	i aerosinothos
(male)	ο αεροσυνοδός	o aerosinothos
flight number	ο αριθμός πτήσεως	o ariTHmos ptiseos
gate	η έξοδος	i exothos

jet	το τζετ	to "jet"
land (verb)	προσγειώνομαι	prosyionome
passport	το διαβατήριο	to thiavatirio
passport control	ο έλεγχος	o elenhos
	διαβατηρίων	thiavatirion
pilot	ο πιλότος	o pilotos
runway	ο διάδρομος	o thiathromos
seat	η θέση	i THesi
seat belt	η ζώνη ασφαλείας	i zoni asfalias
take off (verb)	απογειώνομαι	apoyionome
window	το παράθυρο	to paraTHiro
wing	το φτερό	to ftero

When is there a flight to . . . ?
Πότε έχει πτήση για . . . ;
pote ehi ptisi ya

What time does the flight to . . . leave?
Τί ώρα φεύγει η πτήση για . . . ;
ti ora fevyi i ptisi ya

Is it a direct flight?
Υπάρχει κατευθείαν πτήση;
iparhi katefTHian ptisi

Do I have to change planes?
Πρέπει ν'αλλάξω αεροπλάνο;
prepi nalaxo aeroplano

When do I have to check in?
Πότε πρέπει να δώσω τις αποσκευές μου;
pote prepi na thoso tis aposkeves moo

I'd like a one-way/round-trip ticket to . . .
Θα ήθελα ένα απλό/μετ'επιστροφής εισιτήριο γιά . . .
THa iTHela ena aplo/metepistrofis isitirio ya

I'd like a nonsmoking seat, please
Θέλω μία θέση στους μη καπνίζοντες, παρακαλώ
THElo mia THEsi stoos mi kapnizondes, parakalo

I'd like a window seat, please
Θέλω μία θέση με παράθυρο, παρακαλώ
THElo mia THEsi me paraTHIro, parakalo

How long will the flight be delayed?
Ποσο θα καθυστερήσει η πτήση;
poso THA kaTHisterisi i ptisi

Is this the right gate for the . . . flight?
Αυτή είναι η σωστή έξοδος γιά την πτήση . . . ;
afti ine i sosti exothos ya tin ptisi

When do we arrive in . . . ?
Πότε φτάνουμε . . . ;
pote ftanoome

May I smoke now?
Επιτρέπετε να καπνίσω τώρα;
epitrepete na kapniso tora

I do not feel very well
Δεν αισθάνομαι καλά
THen esTHanome kala

THINGS YOU'LL SEE OR HEAR

OA	*Olimbiaki*	Olympic Airways
αεροδρόμιο	*aerothromio*	airport
αερολιμήν	*aerolimin*	airport
αεροσυνοδός	*aerosinothos*	flight attendant
αναχωρίσεις	*anahorisis*	departures
απαγορεύεται το κάπνισμα	*apagorevete to kapnisma*	no smoking
αφίξεις	*afixis*	arrivals
διάδρομος	*thiathromos*	runway
διάρκεια πτήσεως	*thiarkia ptiseos*	flight time
δρομολόγια	*thromologyia*	timetable
έλεγχος διαβατηρίων	*elenhos thiavatirion*	passport control
έξοδος	*exothos*	exit, gate, door
έξοδος κινδύνου	*exothos kinthinoo*	emergency exit
επιβάτες	*epivates*	passengers
κυβερνήτης	*kivernitis*	captain
πληροφορίες	*plirofories*	information
πλήρωμα	*pliroma*	crew
προσδεθήτε	*pros-theTHite*	fasten your seat belt
πτήσεις εξωτερικού	*ptisis exoterikoo*	international flights
πτήσεις εσωτερικού	*ptisis esoterikoo*	domestic flights
τοπική ώρα	*topiki ora*	local time
ύψος	*ipsos*	altitude

BUS, TAXI, AND SUBWAY TRAVEL

All Greek cities have a good bus system. Most buses are one-man operated, and you pay the driver as you enter. In Athens there are electric trolleys in addition to the bus services. In the early morning, from 6 to 8 or 9 AM, the bus service is free.

The main towns are connected by an excellent system of long-distance buses, which run punctually and more than make up for the less than extensive railroad system. The buses are comfortable, fast, and often have air-conditioning. Tickets are bought at the terminal before boarding for the long-distance services.

Taxis are plentiful in Greece, less expensive than in western Europe and much more frequently used. They are yellow or sometimes gray and are marked TAXI. For short local trips you pay by the kilometer, and the fare is displayed on the meter. For longer drives, ask what the fare is in advance.

Only Athens has a subway system, which is called Ο ΗΛΕΚΤΡΙΚΟΣ (*o ilektrikos*) and which joins Piraeus with Athens and Kifisia.

USEFUL WORDS AND PHRASES

bus	το λεωφορείο	*to leoforio*
(*long distance*)	το πούλμαν	*to poolman*
bus stop	η στάση	*i stasi*
child	το παιδί	*to pethi*
conductor	ο εισπράκτορας	*o ispraktoras*
connection	η σύνδεση	*i sinthesi*
driver	ο οδηγός	*o othigos*
fare	η τιμή	*i timi*
lake	η λίμνη	*i limni*
number 5 bus	το πέντε	*to pende*
passenger	ο επιβάτης	*o epivatis*
port	το λιμάνι	*to limani*
river	το ποτάμι	*to potami*
sea	η θάλασσα	*i THalasa*

seat	η θέση	i THesi
station	ο σταθμός	o staTHmos
subway	ο ηλεκτρικός	o ilektrikos
taxi	το ταξί	to taxi
ticket	το εισιτήριο	to isitirio

Where is the nearest subway station?
Που είναι ο πλησιέστερος σταθμός του ηλεκτρικού;
poo ine o plisi-esteros staTHmos too ilektrikoo

Where is the bus station?
Που είναι ο σταθμός των υπεραστικών λεωφορίων;
poo ine o staTHmos ton iperastikon leoforion

Where is the bus stop?
Που είναι η στάση;
poo ine i stasi

Which buses go to . . . ?
Ποιά λεωφορεία πάνε στο . . . ;
pia leoforia pane sto

How often do the buses to . . . run?
Πόσο συχνά έχει λεωφορείο γιά . . . ;
poso sihna ehi leoforio ya

Would you tell me when we get to . . . ?
Μπορείτε να μου πείτε πότε φτάνουμε στο . . . ;
borite na moo pite pote ftanoome sto

Do I get off here?
Πρέπει να κατέβω εδώ;
prepi na katevo etho

How do you get to . . . ?
Πως πάμε στο . . . ;
pos pame sto

Is it very far?
Είναι πολύ μακριά;
ine poli makria

I want to go to . . .
Θέλω να πάω στο . . .
THelo na pao sto

Do you go near . . . ?
Πάτε κοντά στο . . . ;
pate konda sto

Where can I buy a ticket?
Από πού μπορώ ν'αγοράσω ένα εισιτήριο;
apo poo boro nagoraso ena isitirio

Please close/open the window
Παρακαλώ, ανοίγετε/κλείνετε το παράθυρο;
parakalo, aniyete/klinete to paraTHiro

Could you help me get a ticket?
Μπορείτε να με βοηθήσετε να βγάλω ένα εισιτήριο;
borite na me voiTHisete na vgalo ena isitirio

When does the last bus leave?
Πότε φεύγει το τελευταίο λεωφορείο;
pote fevyi to telefteo leofirio

THINGS YOU'LL SEE

Απαγορεύεται η είσοδος	*apagorevete i isothos*	no entry
γραμμή	*grami*	route
εισιτήρια	*isitiria*	tickets
έλεγχος εισιτηρίων	*elenhos isitirion*	ticket inspection
ελεύθερον	*elefTHeron*	for hire (taxis)
ηλεκτρικός	*ilektrikos*	subway
θέσεις	*THesis*	seats
μην ομιλείτε στον οδηγό	*min omilite ston othigo*	do not speak to the driver
οδηγός	*othigos*	driver
ορθίων	*orTHion*	standing
παιδικό	*pethiko*	children
πρόστιμο	*prostimo*	fine (penalty)
πυροσβεστήρ	*pirosvestir*	fire extinguisher
σταθμός ταξί	*staTHmos taxi*	taxi stand
σταθμός υπεραστικών λεωφορείων	*staTHmos iperastikon leoforion*	bus station (long-distance buses)
στάσις	*stasis*	bus stop
ταξί	*taxi*	taxi
ταρίφα	*tarifa*	taxi tariff
χωρητικότητος . . . ατόμων	*horitikotitos . . . atomon*	maximum load . . . persons
χωρις εισπράκτορα	*horis ispraktora*	no ticket collector

RESTAURANTS

Restaurants, bars, and discos are obliged by law to close at 3 AM on weekdays and 4 AM on Saturdays. Children are allowed in places where alcohol is served. Some examples of places to eat and drink are shown below (notice that signs in Greek uppercase letters often look different than the same words in lowercase).

ΕΣΤΙΑΤΟΡΙΟΝ Εστιατόριον *estiatorion* ("restaurant")
In all tourist places you will find the menu printed in English as well as Greek and the staff will almost certainly speak English. If you feel more adventurous, you might prefer to try some of the many Greek delicacies available. In smaller places you will be welcomed into the kitchen to see just what's cooking. In all types of Greek restaurants you are provided with water and bread at no charge. The menu will usually give you two prices for each item—the higher one includes a service charge.

ΤΑΒΕΡΝΑ Ταβέρνα *taverna*
This is a typical Greek restaurant, where wine is available "on tap." (Note that wine is ordered by weight not by volume, so you might order a kilo, not a liter.)

ΨΑΡΟΤΑΒΕΡΝΑ Ψαροταβέρνα *psarotaverna*
A restaurant specializing in seafood.

ΨΗΣΤΑΡΙΑ Ψησταριά *psistaria*
A restaurant specializing in charcoal-grilled food.

ΟΥΖΕΡΙ Ουζερί *oozeri*
A bar that serves ouzo (a strong, anise-flavored alcoholic drink) and beer with snacks (called **mezethes**) served as side dishes. These snacks could be standard appetizers or sometimes, especially in the islands, octopus or local seafood.

ΖΑΧΑΡΟΠΛΑΣΤΕΙΟ Ζαχαροπλαστείο *zaharoplastio*
Pastry shop or café that serves cakes and soft drinks and is
also an ideal place to have breakfast.

ΚΑΦΕΝΕΙΟ Καφενείο *kafenio*
Coffeehouse, where Greek coffee is served with traditional
desserts, and you can play a game of cards or backgammon.
Greek women are rarely seen here.

USEFUL WORDS AND PHRASES

beer	η μπύρα	i bira
bill	ο λογαριασμός	o logariasmos
bottle	το μπουκάλι	to bookali
cake	το γλυκό	to gliko
chef	ο μάγειρας	o mayiras
coffee	ο καφές	o kafes
cup	το φλυτζάνι	to flitzani
fork	το πιρούνι	to pirooni
glass	το ποτήρι	to potiri
knife	το μαχαίρι	to maheri
menu	το μενού	to menoo
milk	το γάλα	to gala
napkin	η χαρτοπετσέτα	i hartopetseta
plate	το πιάτο	to piato
receipt	η απόδειξη	i apothixi
sandwich	το σάντουιτς	to sandooits
soup	η σούπα	i soopa
spoon	το κουτάλι	to kootali
sugar	η ζάχαρη	i zahari
table	το τραπέζι	to trapezi
tea	το τσάι	to tsai
teaspoon	το κουταλάκι	to kootalaki
tip	το πουρμπουάρ	to poorbooar
waiter	ο σερβιτόρος	o servitoros
waitress	η σερβιτόρα	i servitora

water	το νερό	to nero
wine	το κρασί	to krasi
wine list	ο κατάλογος	o katalogos
	κρασιών	krasion

A table for 1/2/3, please
Ένα τραπέζι για ένα/δύο/τρία άτομα, παρακαλώ
ena trapezi ya ena/thio/tria atoma, parakalo

May we see the menu/wine list?
Μπορούμε να δούμε το μενού/τον κατάλογο των κρασιών;
boroome na thoome to menoo/ton katalogo ton krasion

What would you recommend?
Τι θα προτείνατε;
ti THa protinate

I'd like . . .
Θα ήθελα . . .
THa ithela

Just a cup of coffee, please
Μόνο ένα φλυτζάνι καφέ, παρακαλώ
mono ena flitzani kafe, parakalo

A kilo/half a kilo of retsina
Ένα κιλό/μισό κιλό ρετσίνα
ena kilo/miso kilo retsina

Waiter!
Γκαρσόν!
garson

May we have the bill, please?
Μας φέρνετε τον λογαριασμό, παρακαλώ;
mas fernete ton logariasmo, parakalo

I only want a snack
Θέλω κάτι ελαφρύ
THelo kati elafri

I didn't order this
Δεν παράγγειλα αυτό
then parangila afto

May we have some more . . . ?
Μπορούμε να έχουμε ακόμη λίγο . . . ;
boroome na ehoome akomi ligo

The meal was very good, thank you
Το φαγητό ήταν πολύ καλό, ευχαριστούμε
to fayito itan poli kalo, efharistoome

My compliments to the chef!
Τα συγχαρητήριά μου στον μάγειρα!
ta sinharitiria moo ston mayira

MENU GUIDE

αγγινάρες αυγολέμονο	anginares avgolemono	artichokes in egg and lemon sauce
αγγούρια και ντομάτες σαλάτα	angooria ke domates salata	cucumber and tomato salad
αλάτι	alati	salt
αλεύρι καλαμποκιού	alevri kalabokioo	cornstarch
αλεύρι σταριού	alevri starioo	wheat flour
αλλαντικά	alandika	sausages, salami, meats
αμύγδαλα	amigthala	almonds
αμυγδαλωτά	amigthalota	macaroons
ανανάς	ananas	pineapple
ανανάς χυμός	ananas himos	pineapple juice
ανθότυρο	anthotiro	kind of cottage cheese
αντζούγιες στο λάδι	antsooyies sto lathi	anchovies in oil
αρακάς λαδερός	arakas latheros	peas cooked with tomato and oil
αρακάς σωτέ	arakas sote	peas fried in butter
αρνί μπούτι στη λαδόκολα	arni booti sti lathokola	leg of lamb wrapped in greased foil
αρνί γεμιστό στο φούρνο	arni yemisto sto foorno	oven-cooked stuffed lamb
αρνί εξοχικό	arni exohiko	lamb cooked in greased foil with cheese and spices
αρνί κοκκινιστό	arni kokkinisto	lamb in tomato sauce
αρνί λαδορίγανη στο φούρνο	arni lathoriyani sto foorno	oven-cooked lamb with oil and oregano
αρνί με αρακά	arni me araka	lamb with peas
αρνί με κολοκυθάκια αυγολέμονο	arni me kolokithakia avgolemono	lamb with zucchini in egg and lemon sauce
αρνί με κριθαράκι	arni me kritharaki	lamb with rice-shaped pasta
αρνί με μελιτζάνες	arni me melitzanes	lamb with eggplant
αρνί με μπάμιες	arni me bamies	lamb with okra
αρνί με πατάτες ραγκού	arni me patates ragoo	lamb with potatoes cooked in tomato sauce

50

αρνί με φασολάκια φρέσκα	*arni me fasolakia freska*	lamb with beans
αρνί με χυλοπίτες	*arni me hilopites*	lamb with a kind of lasagna
αρνί μπούτι στο φούρνο	*arni booti sto foorno*	oven-cooked leg of lamb
αρνί μπριζόλες	*arni brizoles*	lamb chops
αρνί με μακαρόνια	*arni me makaronia*	lamb with spaghetti
αρνί παιδάκια	*arni paithakia*	grilled lamb chops
αρνί τας κεμπάπ	*arni tas kebab*	chopped lamb kebab with tomato sauce
αρνί της κατσαρόλας με πατάτες	*arni tis katsarolas me patates*	lamb casserole with potatoes
αρνί της σούβλας	*arni tis soovlas*	spit-roasted lamb
αρνί φρικασέ	*arni frikase*	lamb fricassee
αστακός με λαδολέμονο	*astakos me latholemono*	lobster cooked in lemon and oil sauce
αστακός με μαγιονέζα	*astakos me mayoneza*	lobster with mayonnaise
αστακός βραστός	*astakos vrastos*	boiled lobster
ατζέμ πιλάφι	*atzem pilafi*	rice pilaf
αυγά βραστά	*avga vrasta*	boiled eggs
αυγά βραστά σφιχτά	*avga vrasta sfihta*	hard-boiled eggs
αυγά γεμιστά	*avga yemista*	stuffed eggs
αυγά γεμιστά με μαγιονέζα	*avga yemista me mayoneza*	eggs stuffed with mayonnaise mix
αυγά μάτια	*avga matia*	fried eggs
αυγά με μανιτάρια	*avga me manitaria*	mushroom omelette
αυγά με μπέικον	*avga me beykon*	bacon and eggs
αυγά με ντομάτες	*avga me domates*	scrambled eggs with tomatoes
αυγά με τυρί	*avga me tiri*	cheese omelette
αυγά ομελέτα	*avga omeleta*	plain omelette
αυγά ομελέτα με πατάτες	*avga omeleta me patates*	omelette with French fries
αυγά ποσέ	*avga pose*	poached eggs
αυγά ώ γκρατέν	*avga o graten*	eggs au gratin
αυγολέμονο (σούπα)	*avgolemono (soopa)*	egg and lemon soup
αυγοτάραχο	*avgotaraho*	roe
αχλάδι χυμός	*ahlathi himos*	pear juice
αχλαδιά	*ahlathia*	pears

βακαλάος κροκέτες	vakalaos kroketes	haddock croquettes
βερύκοκκα	verikoka	apricots
τάρτα με βερύκοκκα	tarta me verikoka	apricot tart
χυμός βερύκοκκο	himos verikoko	apricot juice
βούτυρο	vootiro	butter
βούτυρο φυστικιού	vootiro fistikioo	peanut butter
βρασμένος, βραστός	vrasmenos, vrastos	boiled
βυσσινάδα	visinatha	black cherry juice
βύσσινο	visino	cherries
βωδινό βραστό	vothino vrasto	boiled beef
βωδινό ροσμπίφ	vothino rosbif	roast beef
βωδινό φιλέτο	vothino fileto	grilled beef steak
στη σχάρα	sti s-hara	
βωδινό ψητό	vothino psito	roast beef cooked in the
στο φούρνο	sto foorno	oven
βωδινός κιμάς	vothinos kimas	ground beef
βωδινό κορν-μπίφ	vothino korn-bif	corned beef
γάβρος στο φούρνο	gavross sto foorno	small type of fish cooked
με ντομάτα	me domata	in the oven with
		tomato sauce
γάβρος τηγανιτός	gavros tiganitos	fried small fish
γάλα	gala	milk
γάλα αγελάδος με λίπος	gala agelathos me lipos	cow's milk with 1% fat
ένα της εκατό	ena tis ekato	
γάλα εβαπορέ	gala evapore	evaporated milk
γάλα σοκολατούχο	gala sokolatooho	chocolate milk
γάλα συμπηκνωμένο	gala sibiknomeno	sweet evaporated milk
ζαχαρούχο	zaharooho	
γαλακτομπούρεκο	galaktobooreko	cream pie with honey
γαλέος τηγανητός	galeos tiganitos	fried cod with
σκορδαλιά	skorthalia	garlic sauce
γαλλικός καφές	galikos kafes	French (filtered) coffee
γαλοπούλα ψητή στο	galopoola psiti sto	roast turkey
φούρνο	foorno	
γαλοπούλα γεμιστή	galopoola yemisti	stuffed turkey
γαλοπούλα κοκκινιστή	galopoola kokinisti	turkey cooked with
		tomatoes
γαρίδες καναπέ	garithes kanape	shrimp canapés
γαρδούμπα	garthooba	lamb's intestines
		on the spit

γαρίδες βραστές	garithes vrastes	boiled shrimps
γαρίδες κοκτέιλ	garithes kokteyl	shrimp cocktail
γαρίδες πιλάφι	garithes pilafi	shrimp pilaf
γαρνιτούρα με καρότα σωτέ	garnitoora me karota sote	sautéed carrots
γαρνιτούρα με κουνουπίδι σωτέ	garnitoora me kounoupithi sote	sautéed cauliflower
γαρνιτούρα πατάτες	garnitoora patates	potatoes
γαρνιτούρα με σπανάκι σωτέ	garnitoora me spanaki sote	sautéed spinach
γαρνιτούρα φασόλια πράσινα σωτέ	garnitoora fasolia prasina sote	sautéed beans
γαρνιτούρα με φασόλια ξερά σωτέ	garnitoora me fasolia xera sote	sautéed lima beans
γιαλατζή ντολμάδες	yalantzi dolmathes	vine leaves stuffed with rice
γιαούρτι αγελάδος άπαχο	yaoorti ayelathos apaho	low-fat cow's yogurt
γιαούρτι αγελάδος πλήρες	yaoorti ayelathos plires	full-fat cow's yogurt
γιαούρτι πρόβειο	yaoorti provio	sheep's yogurt
γιαούρτι φρούτων	yaoorti frooton	fruit yogurt
γιουβαρλάκια αυγολέμονο	yioovarlakia avgolemono	meatballs with rice in egg and lemon sauce
γιουβαρλάκια με σάλτσα ντομάτας	yioovarlakia me saltsa domatas	meatballs with rice cooked with tomatoes
γιουβέτσι	yoovetsi	oven-cooked lamb with a kind of pasta
γκοφρέττα	gofreta	chocolate wafer
γκρέϊπ φρουτ	"grapefruit"	grapefruit
γκρέϊπ φρουτ χυμός	"grapefruit" himos	grapefruit juice
γλυκό μελιτζανάκι	gliko melitzanaki	eggplant preserve in syrup
γλυκό βύσσινο	gliko visino	cherry preserve in syrup
γλυκό καρυδάκι φρέσκο	gliko karithaki fresko	green walnut preserve in syrup
γλυκό μαστίχα	gliko mastiha	vanilla-flavored fudge
γλυκό νεραντζάκι	gliko nerantzaki	bitter orange in syrup
γλυκό σύκο φρέσκο	gliko siko fresko	fig preserve in syrup
γλυκό τριαντάφυλλο	gliko triadafilo	dried rose petal preserve

MENU GUIDE

γλώσσες	gloses	sole
γλώσσες τηγανητές	gloses tiganites	fried sole
γόπα τηγανητή	gopa tiganiti	type of fried fish
γουρουνόπουλο στο φούρνο με πατάτες	gooroonopoolo sto foorno me patates	oven-cooked pork with potatoes
γραβιέρα τυρί	graviera tiri	kind of savory cheese
γρανίτα από λεμόνι	granita apo lemoni	lemon sorbet
γρανίτα από μπανάνα	granita apo banana	banana sorbet
γρανίτα από πορτοκάλι	granita apo portokali	orange sorbet
γρανίτα από φράουλες	granita apo fraooles	strawberry sorbet
δαμάσκηνα	thamaskina	prunes
δίπλες, τηγανητές	thiples, tiganites	pancakes
εκλαίρ σοκολάτας	ekler sokolatas	chocolate éclair
ελαιόλαδο	eleolatho	olive oil
ελιές	elies	olives
ελληνικός καφές	elinikos kafes	Greek coffee
εντόστια αρνιού λαδορίγανη	entostia arnioo lathorigani	lamb's intestines cooked in lemon and oil
εσκαλόπ με ζαμπόν και σάλτσα ντομάτας	eskalop me zabon ke saltsa domatas	veal scallop with ham and tomato sauce
ζαμπόν	zabon	ham
ζάχαρη μαύρη	zahari mavri	brown sugar
ζάχαρη άσπρη	zahari aspri	white sugar
ζελέ βερύκοκκου	zele verikokkoo	apricot gelatin
ζελέ κεράσι	zele kerasi	cherry gelatin
ζελέ πορτοκαλιού	zele portokalioo	orange gelatin
ζελέ φράουλα	zele fraoola	strawberry gelatin
ζυμαρικά	zimarika	pasta
ζωμός κότας/κρέατος/ λαχανικών	zomos kotas/kreatos/ lahanikon	chicken/beef/vegetable stock
ηλιέλαιο	ilieleo	sunflower oil
θαλασσινά	thalassina	seafood
καβούρια ψητά	kavooria psita	grilled crab
κακαβιά ψαρόσουπα	kakavia psarosoopa	fish soup
κακάο	kakao	cocoa
κακάο ρόφημα	kakao rofima	hot chocolate
καλαμαράκια γεμιστά	kalamarakia yemista	stuffed squid
καλαμαράκια τηγανητά	kalamarakia tiganita	fried squid
καλαμποκέλαιο	kalabokeleo	corn oil

καλαμπόκι	kalaboki	corn
καναπέ με ζαμπόν	kanape me zabon	ham canapés
καναπέ με κρέας ψητό	kanape me kreas psito	cooked meat canapés
καναπέ με μαύρο χαβιάρι	kanape me mavro haviari	black caviar canapés
καναπέ με ταραμοσαλάτα	kanape me taramosalata	taramosalata canapés
κανελλόνια γεμιστά	kanelonia yemista	stuffed canelloni
καπαμάς αρνί	kapamas arni	lamb cooked in spices and tomato sauce
καραβίδες	karavithes	prawns
καραμέλες	karameles	sweets
καρμπονάρα	karbonara	spaghetti carbonara
καρότα	karota	carrots
καρπούζι	karpoozi	watermelon
καρύδα	karitha	coconut
καρύδια	karithia	walnuts
καρυδόπιττα	karithopita	cake with nuts and syrup
κασέρι	kaseri	type of Greek cheese
κάστανα	kastana	chestnuts
κάστανα γκλασέ	kastana glase	glazed chestnuts
καταΐφι	kataifi	honey and nut dessert
καφές βαρύς γλυκός	kafes varis glikos	sweet Greek coffee
καφές με γάλα	kafes me gala	coffee with milk
καφές μέτριος	kafes metrios	medium sweet Greek coffee
κέϊκ κανέλλας	keik kanelas	cinnamon cake
κέϊκ με αμύγδαλα	keik me amigdala	almond cake
κέϊκ με καρύδια και σταφίδες	keik me karithia ke stafithes	nut and sultana cake
κέϊκ σοκολάτας	keik sokolatas	chocolate cake
κέϊκ φρούτων	keik frooton	fruit cake
κεράσια	kerasia	cherries
κέτσαπ	ketsap	ketchup
κέφαλος	kefalos	mullet
κεφαλοτύρι	kefalotiri	type of Greek parmesan-style cheese
κεφτέδες τηγανητοί	keftethes tiganiti	fried meatballs
κεφτέδες με σάλτσα	keftethes me saltsa	meatballs in tomato sauce

κεφτέδες στο φούρνο	*keftethes sto foorno*	oven-cooked meatballs
κόκα κόλα	*koka kola*	Coca Cola®
κοκορέτσι	*kokoretsi*	spit-roasted lamb's intestines
κολιοί ψητοί	*koli-i psiti*	fried mackerel
κολοκυθάκια γεμιστά με ρύζι	*kolokiTHakia yemista me rizi*	zucchini stuffed with rice and ground meat
κολοκυθάκια λαδερά	*kolokiTHakia lathera*	zucchini cooked in oil
κολοκυθάκια σαλάτα	*kolokiTHakia salata*	zucchini salad
κολοκυθάκια τηγανητά	*kolokiTHakia tiganita*	fried zucchini
κολοκυθοκεφτέδες	*kolokiTHokeftethes*	fried zucchini balls
κολοκυθοτυρόπιττα	*kolokiTHotiropita*	zucchini and cheese pie
κολοκυθάκια γεμιστά με κιμά	*kolokiTHakia yemista me kima*	zucchini stuffed with ground meat
κολοκυθάκια με πατάτες	*kolokiTHakia me patates*	zucchini with potatoes
κολοκυθάκια μουσακάς	*kolokiTHakia mousakas*	zucchini with ground meat and béchamel sauce
κολοκυθάκια παπουτσάκι	*kolokiTHakia papootsaki*	zucchini with ground meat and onions
κομπόστα με βερύκοκκα	*kobosta me verikoka*	apricot compote
κομπόστα με μήλα	*komposta me mila*	apple compote
κομπόστα με ροδάκινα	*komposta me rothakina*	peach compote
κορν φλέϊκς	*korn fleiks*	cornflakes
κότα βραστή	*kota vrasti*	boiled chicken
κότα γεμιστή	*kota yemisti*	stuffed chicken
κότα κοκκινιστή	*kota kokkinisti*	chicken in tomato sauce
κότα ψητή στο φούρνο	*kota psiti sto foorno*	roast chicken
κότα ψητή σούβλας	*kota psiti soovlas*	spit-roasted chicken
κότα ψητή της κατσαρόλας	*kota psiti tis katsarolas*	roast chicken in the pot
κοτολέτες αρνίσιες πανέ	*kotoletes arnisies pane*	lamb cutlets

κοτολέτες μοσχαρίσιες πανέ	kotoletes mos-harisies pane	veal cutlets
κοτόπιττα	kotopita	chicken pie
κοτόπουλο γιουβέτσι με χυλοπίττες	kotopoolo yioovetsi me hilopites	chicken with a kind of pasta
κοτόπουλο με μπάμιες	kotopoolo me bamies	chicken with okra
κοτόπουλο με μπιζέλια	kotopoolo me bizelia	chicken with peas
κοτόπουλο πανέ	kotopoolo pane	breaded chicken
κοτόπουλο πιλάφι	kotopoolo pilafi	chicken pilaf
κοτόσουπα	kotosoopa	chicken soup
κουκιά λαδερά	kookia lathera	broad beans in tomato sauce
κουλούρια κανέλλας/ με σουσάμι	koolooria kanelas/ me soosami	cinnamon/sesame cookies
κουνέλι με σάλτσα	kooneli me saltsa	rabbit with tomato sauce
κουνέλι στιφάδο	kooneli stifatho	rabbit with onions
κουνουπίδι βραστό σαλάτα	koonoopithi vrasto salata	boiled cauliflower salad
κουραμπιέδες με αμύγδαλο	koorabiethes me amigthalo	shortbread with nuts and icing
κράκερς αλμυρά	krakers almira	crackers
κρασί	krasi	wine
κρασί άσπρο	krasi aspro	white wine
κρασί κόκκινο	krasi kokino	red wine
κρασί μαυροδάφνη	krasi mavrothafni	sweet red wine
κρασί ρετσίνα	krasi retsina	dry white Greek wine
κρασί ροζέ	krasi roze	rosé
κρέας με αντίδια αυγολέμονο	kreas me antithia avgolemono	beef with endive in egg and lemon sauce
κρέας με φασόλια ξερά	kreas me fasolia xera	beef with lima beans
κρεατόπιττες	kreatopites	ground meat pies
κρέμα καραμελέ	krema karamele	crème caramel
κρέμα με μήλα	krema me mila	apples with cream
κρέμα με μπανάνες	krema me bananes	bananas with cream
κρεμμυδάκια φρέσκα	kremithakia freska	scallions
κρεμμύδια	kremithia	onions
κρεμμυδόσουπα	kremithosoopa	onion soup

κροκέτες απο κρέας	kroketes apo kreas	meat croquettes
κροκέτες με αυγά και τυρί	kroketes me avga ke tiri	croquettes with egg and cheese
κροκέτες με μπακαλιάρο	kroketes me bakaliaro	cod croquettes
κροκέτες με πατάτα	kroketes me patata	potato croquettes
κρουασάν	krooasan	croissants
κυδωνόπαστο	kithonopasto	thick quince gelatin
κωκ	kok	cream cake with chocolate topping
λαγός με σάλτσα	lagos me saltsa	hare in tomato sauce
λαγός στιφάδο	lagos stifatho	hare with onions
λάδι	lathi	oil
λαζάνια	lazania	lasagna
λαχανάκια Βρυξελλών	lahanaka vrixelon	Brussels sprouts
λαχανάκια μικτά	lahanika mikta	mixed vegetables
λάχανο	lahano	cabbage
λάχανο κόκκινο	lahano kokino	red cabbage
λάχανο ντολμάδες αυγολέμονο	lahano dolmathes avgolemono	stuffed cabbage leaves in egg and lemon sauce
λάχανο ντολμάδες με σάλτσα ντομάτας	lahano dolmathes me saltsa domatas	stuffed vine leaves in tomato sauce
λαχανοσαλάτα	lahanosalata	cabbage salad
λεμόνι	lemoni	lemon
χυμός λεμονιού	himos lemonioo	lemon juice
λιθρίνι ψητό	liтнrini psito	grilled mullet
λουκάνικα βραστά	lookanika vrasta	boiled sausages
λουκάνικα καπνιστά στη σχάρα	lookanika kapnista sti s-hara	smoked sausages on the grill
λουκάνικα τηγανητά	lookanika tiganita	fried sausages
λουκουμάδες	lookoomathes	doughnuts
λουκούμια	lookoomia	Turkish delight
μαγειρίτσα	mayiritsa	Easter soup with lamb's intestines
μαγιά	mayia	yeast
μαγιονέζα	mayoneza	mayonnaise
μαϊντανός	maidanos	parsley
μακαρονάκι κοφτό	makaronaki kofto	macaroni
μακαρόνια με κιμά	makaronia me kima	spaghetti Bolognese

μακαρόνια με φρέσκο βουτυρο και παρμεζάνα	makaronia me fresko vootiro ke parmezana	spaghetti with fresh butter and parmesan cheese
μακαρόνια παστίτσιο με κιμά	makaronia pastitsio me kima	spaghetti with rice and béchamel sauce
μανιτάρια	manitaria	mushrooms
μανιτάρια τηγανητά	manitaria tiganita	fried mushrooms
μανταρίνι	madarini	tangerine
μαργαρίνη	margarini	margarine
μαρίδες τηγανητές	marithes tiganites	small fried fish
μαρμελάδα βερύκοκκο	marmelatha verikoko	apricot jam
μαρμελάδα πορτοκάλι	marmelatha portokali	orange jam
μαρμελάδα ροδάκινο	marmelatha rothakino	peach jam
μαρμελάδα φράουλα	marmelatha fraoola	strawberry jam
μαρούλια σαλάτα	maroolia salata	lettuce salad
μέλι	meli	honey
μελιτζάνες γιαχνί	melitzanes yahni	eggplant in tomato and onions
μελιτζάνες παπουτσάκι	melitzanes papootsaki	eggplant cooked with ground meat and tomato
μελιτζάνες γεμιστές με κιμά	melitzanes yemistes me kima	eggplant stuffed with ground meat
μελιτζάνες ιμάμ μπαϊλντί	melitzanes imam baildi	eggplant in garlic and tomato
μελιτζάνες μουσακάς	melitzanes moosakas	eggplant in ground meat, potato, and béchamel sauce
μελιτζάνες τηγανητές	melitzanes tiganites	fried eggplant
μελιτζάνοσαλάτα	melitzanosalata	eggplant salad
μελομακάρονα	melomakarona	sweet cakes with cinnamon, nuts, and syrup
μήλα	mila	apples
μήλα γεμιστά	mila yemista	stuffed apples with cinnamon
μηλόπιττα	milopita	apple pie
μηλοχυμός	milohimos	apple juice
μοσχάρι βραστό	mos-hari vrasto	veal stew

μοσχάρι κοκκινιστό	mos-hari kokkinisto	veal in tomato sauce
μοσχάρι με κριθαράκι	mos-hari me kriTHaraki	veal with rice-shaped pasta
μοσχάρι με μελιτζάνες	mos-hari me melitzanes	veal with eggplant
μοσχάρι με μπάμιες	mos-hari me bamies	veal with okra
μοσχάρι με πατάτες	mos-hari me patates	veal with potatoes
μοσχάρι με πατάτες στο φούρνο	mos-hari me patates sto foorno	veal with potatoes cooked in the oven
μοσχάρι με πουρέ	mos-hari me poore	veal with mashed potatoes
μοσχάρι ροσμπίφ	mos-hari rosbif	roast beef
μοσχάρι με αρακά	mos-hari me araka	veal with peas
μοσχάρι σνίτσελ με πατάτες τηγανές	mos-hari snitzel me patates tiganites	steak and French fries
μοσχάρι σνίτσελ με πουρέ	mos-hari snitzel me poore	steak with mashed potatoes
μοσχαρίσιος κιμάς	mos-harisios kimas	ground beef
μουσακά	moosaka	moussaka
μουσακάς με πατάτες	moosakas me patates	potatoes with ground meat and béchamel sauce
μουστοκούλουρα	moostokooloora	kind of Greek cookies
μουστάρδα	moostartha	mustard
μπακαλιάρος πλακί	bakaliaros plaki	salted cod cooked in tomato sauce
μπακαλιάρος τηγανητός	bakaliaros tiganitos	fried salt cod
μπακλαβάς	baclavas	layers of phyllo pastry with nuts and syrup
μπάμιες λαδερές	bamies latheres	okra with tomato in oil
μπανάνα	banana	banana
μπαρμπούνια πανέ	barboonia pane	breaded red mullet
μπεζέδες	bezethes	meringues with cream
μπέικον καπνιστό	beikon kapnisto	smoked bacon
μπεσαμέλ σάλτσα	besamel saltsa	béchamel sauce
μπισκότα σοκολάτας	biskota sokolatas	chocolate cookies
μπισκοτάκια αλμυρά	biskotakia almira	savory crackers
μπιφτέκι	bifteki	grilled meatballs
μπον φιλέ	bon file	fillet steak
μπουγάτσα γλυκιά	boogatsa glikia	puff pastry with cream filling and icing

μπουρεκάκια	boorekakia	cheese or ground meat pies
μπριάμι με κολοκυθάκια	briami me kolokiтнakia	zucchini cooked with potatoes in the oven
μπριζόλες βωδινές στη σχάρα	brizoles vothines sti s-hara	grilled T-bone steak
μπριζόλες στο τηγάνι	brizoles sto tigani	fried T-bone steak
μπριζόλες χοιρινές	brizoles hirines	pork chops
μπρόκολο	brokolo	broccoli
μπύρα	bira	beer
μυαλά πανέ	miala pane	breaded cow's brains
μύδια τηγανητά	mithia tiganita	fried mussels
νες καφέ	nes kafe	any instant coffee
νεφρά ψητά/τηγανητά	nefra psita /tiganita	grilled/fried kidneys
ντολμάδες αυγολέμονο με κιμά	dolmathes avgolemono me kima	vine leaves stuffed with rice and ground meat in egg and lemon sauce
ντολμάδες γιαλαντζή	dolmathes yialantzi	stuffed vine leaves with rice
ντοματόσουπα	domatosoopa	tomato soup
χυμός ντομάτα	himos domata	tomato juice
ντομάτες γεμιστές με κιμά	domates yemistes me kima	tomatoes stuffed with rice and ground meat
ντοματοσαλάτα	domatosalata	tomato salad
ντομάτα	domata	tomato
ντομάτες γεμιστές με ρύζι	domates yemistes me rizi	stuffed tomatoes with rice
ντόνατς	donats	doughnuts
ξηροί καρποί	xiri karpi	all types of nuts
ξιφίας	xifias	swordfish
ξύδι	xithi	vinegar
ομελέτα	omeleta	omelette
ομελέτα με λουκάνικα	omeleta me lookanika	omelette with sausages
ορεκτικά	orektika	appetizers
ούζο	oozo	ouzo
παγωτό κοκτέϊλ	pagoto kokteil	ice cream sundae
παγωτό κρέμα	pagoto krema	vanilla ice cream
παγωτό βερύκοκκο	pagoto verikoko	apricot ice cream
παγωτό με σαντυγί	pagoto me sandiyi	ice cream with whipped cream

MENU GUIDE

παγωτό μόκκα	pagoto moka	coffee ice cream
παγωτό μπανάνα	pagoto banana	banana ice cream
παγωτό παρφαί	pagoto parfe	ice cream parfait
παγωτό πραλίνα	pagoto pralina	praline ice cream
παγωτό σοκολάτα	pagoto sokolata	chocolate ice cream
παγωτό φράουλα	pagoto fraoola	strawberry ice cream
παγωτό φυστίκι	pagoto fistiki	pistachio ice cream
πάπρικα	paprika	paprika
πάστα αμυγδάλου	pasta amigdaloo	almond gâteau
πάστα κορμός	pasta kormos	chocolate log
πάστα νουγκατίν	pasta nookatin	cream gâteau
πάστα σοκολατίνα	pasta sokolatina	chocolate gâteau
πάστα φράουλα	pasta fraoola	strawberry gâteau
παστίτσιο λαζάνια	pastitsio lazania	lasagna
παστίτσιο μακαρόνια με κιμά	pastitsio makaronia me kima	macaroni and ground meat cooked in the oven with béchamel
πατάτες γαρνιτούρα	patates garnitoora	potatoes
πατάτες γιαχνί	patates yahni	potatoes cooked with onion and tomato
πατάτες με κολοκυθάκια στο φούρνο	patates ke kolokiтнakia sto foorno	potatoes, zucchini, and tomatoes cooked in the oven
πατάτες με κολοκύθια μουσακάς	patates ke kolokiтнia moosakas	potatoes with zucchini, ground meat, and cheese sauce
πατάτες πουρέ	patates poore	mashed potatoes
πατάτες σουφλέ	patates soofle	potato soufflé
πατάτες στο φούρνο ριγανάτες	patates sto foorno riganates	potatoes baked in the oven with oregano, lemon, and olive oil
πατάτες τηγανητές	patates tiganites	French fries
πατάτες τσιπς	patates tsips	potato chips
πατατοσαλάτα	patatosalata	potato salad
πατζάρια	patzaria	beets
πατσάς σούπα	patsas soopa	tripe soup
πεπόνι	peponi	melon
πέστροφα ψητή	pestrofa psiti	grilled trout
πηχτή	pihti	headcheese
πιλάφι με γαρίδες	pilafi me garithes	shrimp pilaf

πιλάφι με μύδια	pilafi me mithia	rice with mussels
πιλάφι με σάλτσα ντομάτα	pilafi me saltsa domata	rice with tomato sauce
πιλάφι τας-κεμπάπ	pilafi tas-kebab	rice with cubes of beef in tomato sauce
πιπέρι	piperi	pepper
πιπεριές γεμιστές με ρύζι/κιμά	piperies yemistes me rizi/kima	peppers stuffed with rice/ground meat
πιπεριές πράσινες/κόκκινες	piperies prasines/kokines	green/red peppers
πιπεριές τηγανητές	piperies tiganites	fried peppers
πιροσκί	piroski	ground meat or sausage rolls
πίτσα με ζαμπόν	pitsa me zabon	ham pizza
πίτσα με μανιτάρια	pitsa me manitaria	mushroom pizza
πίτσα με ντομάτα και τυρί	pitsa me domata ke tiri	cheese and tomato pizza
πίτσα σπέσιαλ	pitsa spesial	special pizza
πίττα με κιμά	pita me kima	ground meat pie
πορτοκαλάδα	portokalatha	orange juice
πορτοκάλι	portokali	orange
χυμός πορτοκάλι	himos portokali	orange juice
πουτίγκα με ανανά	pootiga me anana	pineapple pudding
πουτίγκα με καρύδια	pootiga me karithia	pudding with walnuts
πουτίγκα με σταφίδες	pootiga me stafithes	raisin pudding
πρασσόπιττα	prasopita	leek pie
πράσσα	prasa	leeks
παρμεζάνα	parmezana	parmesan cheese
ραβιόλια	raviolia	ravioli
ραβανί	ravani	very sweet sponge cake
ρίγανη	rigani	oregano
ροδάκινα	rothakina	peaches
ροσμπίφ αρνί μοσχάρι	rozbif arni mos-hari	roast beef, veal, or lamb
ρυζόγαλο	rizogalo	rice pudding
ρώσικη σαλάτα	rosiki salata	vegetable salad
σαλάμι	salami	salami
σαλάτα	salata	salad
σαλάτα αμπελοφάσουλα	salata abelofasoola	bean salad
σαλάτα με κουνουπίδι βραστό	salata me koonoopithi vrasto	boiled cauliflower salad

σαλάτα με μαρούλια	salata me maroolia	lettuce salad
σαλάτα με ντομάτες και αγγούρια	salata me domates ke agooria	tomato and cucumber salad
σαλάτα με ντομάτες και πιπεριές	salata me domates ke piperies	tomato and green pepper salad
σαλάτα με σπαράγγια	salata me sparagia	asparagus salad
σαλάτα με φασόλια ξερά	salata me fasolia xera	lima bean salad
σαλάτα με χόρτα βρασμένα	salata me horta vrasmena	chicory salad
σαλάτα χωριάτικη	salata horiatiki	Greek salad—tomatoes, cucumber, feta cheese, peppers, and olives
σαλιγκάρια	saligaria	snails
σάλτσα μπεσαμέλ	saltsa besamel	béchamel sauce
σάλτσα ντομάτα	saltsa domata	tomato sauce
σαμάλι	samali	semolina cake with honey
σαντιγή	sandiyi	whipped cream
σαρδέλλες λαδιού	sartheles lathioo	sardines in oil
σέλινο	selino	celery
σιμιγδάλη	simigthali	semolina
σιρόπι	siropi	syrup
σκορδαλιά με ψωμί	skorthalia me psomi	thick garlic sauce with bread
σκόρδο	skortho	garlic
σοκολάτα	sokolata	chocolate
σοκολατάκια	sokolatakia	milk chocolates
σολομός καπνιστός	solomos kapnistos	smoked salmon
σουβλάκι καλαμάκι	soovlaki kalamaki	shish kebab
σουβλάκι ντονέρ με πίττα	soovlaki doner me pita	spit-roasted kebab with pita bread
σουβλάκια απο κρέας μοσχαρίσιο	soovlakia apo kreas mos-harisio	veal kebab
σουβλάκια απο κρέας αρνίσιο	soovlakia apo kreas arnisio	lamb kebab
σουβλάκια απο κρέας χοιρινό	soovlakia apo kreas hirino	pork kebab
σούπα ρεβύθια	soopa reviTHia	chickpea soup
σούπα τραχανάς	soopa trahanas	milk broth with flour
σούπα φακές	soopa fakes	lentil soup

σούπα ψάρι/ ψαρόσουπα αυγολέμονο	soopa psari/psarosoopa avgolemono	fish soup with egg and lemon
σουπιές τηγανητές	soopies tiganites	fried cuttlefish
σουσάμι	soosami	sesame
σουτζουκάκια	sootzookakia	spicy meatballs in red sauce
σουφλέ με ζαμπόν	soofle me zabon	ham soufflé
σπαγέτο με φρέσκο βούτυρο και παρμεζάνα	spageto me fresko vootiro ke parmezana	spaghetti with fresh butter and parmesan cheese
σπαράγγια σαλάτα	sparangia salata	asparagus salad
σπληνάντερο	splinandero	intestines stuffed with spleen
σταφίδες	stafithes	raisins
σταφιδόψωμο	stafithopsomo	raisin bread
σταφύλι χυμός	stafili himos	grape juice
σταφύλια	stafilia	grapes
στιφάδο	stifatho	chopped meat in onions
στρείδια	strithia	oysters
σύκα	sika	figs
συκωτάκια μαρινάτα	sikotakia marinata	liver cooked in rosemary
συκωτάκια πιλάφι	sikotakia pilafi	liver pilaf
συκωτάκια στη σχάρα	sikotakia sti s-hara	broiled liver
συκωτάκια τηγανητά	sikotakia tiganita	fried liver
συναγρίδα ψητή	sinagritha psiti	broiled sea bream
σφυρίδα βραστή	sfiritha vrasti	boiled pike
ταραμοκεφτέδες	taramokeftethes	roe pâté balls with spices
ταραμοσαλάτα	taramosalata	roe pâté
τάρτα με κεράσια	tarta me kerasia	cherry tart
τάρτα με κρέμα και αμύγδαλα	tarta me krema ke amigthala	cream and almond tart
τάρτα με κρέμα και καρύδια	tarta me krema ke karithia	cream and walnut tart
τάρτα με φράουλες	tarta me fraooles	strawberry tart
τάρτα μήλου	tarta miloo	apple tart
τας-κεμπάπ	tas kebab	spicy lamb cutlets
τας-κεμπάπ πιλάφι	tas kebab pilafi	spicy lamb cutlets pilaf
τζατζίκι	tzatziki	yogurt, cucumber, garlic, dried mint, and olive oil
τηγανητός	tiganitos	fried

τηγανήτες	tiganites	pancakes
τονοσαλάτα	tonosalata	tuna salad
τόνος	tonos	tuna
τοστ κλαμπ	tost klab	toasted club sandwich
τοστ με αυγό/ζαμπόν/ τυρί/κοτόπουλο	tost me avgo/zabon/ tiri/kotopoolo	toasted sandwich with egg/ham/cheese/chicken
τοστ με κρέας/ μπιφτέκι	tost me kreas/bifteki	toasted sandwich with meat/hamburger
τούρτα αμυγδάλου	toorta amigdaloo	almond gâteau
τούρτα κρέμα με φράουλες	toorta krema me fraooles	gâteau with strawberries and cream
τούρτα μόκκα	toorta moka	coffee gâteau
τούρτα νουγκατίνα	toorta noogatina	nougat gâteau
τούρτα σαντυγί	toorta sandiyi	whipped cream gâteau
τούρτα σοκολάτας	toorta sokolatas	chocolate gâteau
τρουφάκια	troofakia	small chocolate balls
τσάι	tsai	tea
τσιπούρες ψητές	tsipoores psites	roast flatfish
τσίπουρο	tsipooro	kind of ouzo
τσουρέκια	tsoorekia	sweet Easter bread with fresh butter
τυρί	tiri	cheese
τυρόπιττα	tiropita	cheese pie
τυροπιττάκια	tiropitakia	small cheese pies
φάβα	fava	lentils
φασολάδα	fasolatha	thick bean soup
φασολάκια λαδερά	fasolakia lathera	beans in oil
φασολάκια φρέσκα γιαχνί	fasolakia freska yahni	beans with onions and tomato
φασολάκια φρέσκα σαλάτα	fasolakia freska salata	bean salad
φασόλια γίγαντες γιαχνί	fasolia yigades yahni	lima beans with onion and tomato
φασόλια γίγαντες στο φούρνο	fasolia yigades sto foorno	oven-cooked lima beans
φέτα	feta	feta cheese
φιλέ μινιόν	file minion	thin fillet steak
φιλέτο	fileto	fillet steak
φοντάν αμυγδάλου	fodan amigthaloo	almond candy
φοντάν απο καρύδια	fodan apo karithia	walnut candy

φοντάν ινδικής καρύδας	*fodan inthikis karithas*	coconut candy
φουντούκι	*foodooki*	hazelnut
φράουλες	*fraooles*	strawberries
φράουλες μέ σαντυγί	*fraooles me sandiyi*	strawberries with whipped cream
φρικασέ αρνί	*frikase arni*	lamb cooked in lettuce with cream sauce
φρουί-γκλασέ	*frooi-glase*	dried assorted fruits with sugar
φρουτοσαλάτα	*frootosalata*	fruit salad
φρυγανιές	*friganies*	French toast
φύλλο πίττας	*filo pitas*	thin pastry
φυστίκια	*fistikia*	peanuts
φυστίκια Αιγίνης	*fistikia eyinis*	pistachios
χαβιάρι	*haviari*	caviar
χαλβάς	*halvas*	halvah (candy made from sesame seeds and nuts)
χάμπουργκερ	*hamboorger*	hamburger
χοιρινό με σέλινο	*hirino me selino*	pork casserole with celery
χοιρινό παστό	*hirino pasto*	salted pork
χοιρινό σούβλας	*hirino soovlas*	pork on the spit
χοιρινό στη σχάρα	*hirino sti s-hara*	broiled pork
χοιρινό φούρνου με πατάτες	*hirino foornoo me patates*	roast pork with potatoes
χόρτα βρασμένα σαλάτα	*horta vrasmena salata*	boiled chicory salad
χορτόσουπα	*hortosoopa*	vegetable soup
χταπόδι βραστό	*htapothi vrasto*	boiled octopus
χταπόδι κρασάτο	*htapothi krasato*	octopus in wine
χταπόδι με μακαρονάκι	*htapothi me makaronaki*	octopus with macaroni
χταπόδι πιλάφι	*htapothi pilafi*	octopus pilaf
χταπόδι στιφάδο	*htapothi stifatho*	octopus with small onions
χυλοπίττες με βούτυρο και τυρί	*hilopites me vootiro ke tiri*	tagliatelle with butter and cheese
χυλοπίττες με κοτόπουλο	*hilopites me kotopoolo*	tagliatelle with chicken
χυλοπίττες με κιμά	*hilopites me kima*	tagliatelle with ground meat sauce

χυμός	*himos*	juice
χυμός ντομάτας	*himos domatas*	tomato juice
χωριάτικη σαλάτα	*horiatiki salata*	Greek salad—tomatoes, cucumber, feta cheese, peppers, and olives
ψάρι βραστό μαγιονέζα	*psari vrasto mayoneza*	steamed fish with mayonnaise
ψάρια γλώσσες βραστές με αυγολέμονο	*psaria gloses vrastes me avgolemono*	steamed sole with oil and lemon
ψάρια μαρινάτα	*psaria marinata*	marinated fish
ψάρια τηγανητά	*psaria tiganita*	fried fish
ψάρια ψητά στη σχάρα	*psaria psita sti s-hara*	charcoal-grilled fish
ψαρόσουπα	*psarosoopa*	fish soup
ψητός	*psitos*	broiled
ψωμί άσπρο/μαύρο	*psomi aspro/mavro*	white/brown bread
ψωμί για τοστ	*psomi ya tost*	sliced bread

SHOPPING

The main thing to remember about shopping in Greece is that most stores will be closed for quite a long period during the middle of the day when the sun is at its hottest. Small village stores tend to be open for 12 hours or more a day, but they are liable to be closed from 1 PM until 4 PM. Stores in towns open from 8 AM until 2:30 PM and from 5 PM until 8:30 PM. Stores close on Sundays and public holidays, with the exception of tourist-oriented stores, which tend to be open all week and later in the evening. The Greek institution of the kiosk, or **periptero**, sells items such as cigarettes, candy, stamps, and postcards as well as many of the small items that you might need on a day-to-day basis. It usually has a public telephone too.

USEFUL WORDS AND PHRASES

bakery	ο φούρναρης	*o foornaris*
bookstore	το βιβλιοπωλείο	*to vivliopolio*
boutique	η μπουτίκ	*i bootik*
butcher	ο χασάπης	*o hasapis*
buy (*verb*)	αγοράζω	*agorazo*
cash register	το ταμείο	*to tamio*
drugstore	το φαρμακείο	*to farmakio*
fashion	η μόδα	*i motha*
fish market	το ψαράδικο	*to psarathiko*
florist	το ανθοπωλείο	*to anthopolio*
greengrocer	το μανάβικο	*to manaviko*
grocery store	το μπακάλικο	*to bakaliko*
hardware store	το σιδεράδικο	*to sitherathiko*
inexpensive	φτηνό	*ftino*
ladies' wear	τα γυναικεία	*ta yinekia*
menswear	τα ανδρικά	*ta anthrika*
newsstand	το εφημεριδοπωλείο	*to efimerithopolio*
pastry shop	το ζαχαροπλαστείο	*to zaharoplastio*
pharmacy	το φαρμακείο	*to farmakio*

receipt	η απόδειξη	i *apothixi*
record store	το δισκάδικο	to *thiskathiko*
sales	οι εκπτώσεις	i *ekptosis*
shoe store	το υποδηματοπωλείο	to *ipothimatopolio*
go shopping	πάω για ψώνια	*pao* ya *psonia*
souvenir shop	τουριστικά είδη	*tooristika ithi*
special offer	η τιμή ευκαιρίας	i *timi efkerias*
spend	ξοδεύω	*xothevo*
stationery store	το βιβλιοπωλείο	to *vivliopolio*
store	το μαγαζί	to *magazi*
supermarket	το σούπερ-μάρκετ	to "supermarket"
tailor	ο ράφτης	o *raftis*
toy store	το κατάστημα παιχνιδιών	to *katastima pehnithion*
travel agent	το γραφείο ταξειδίων	to *grafio taxithion*

I'd like . . .
Θα ήθελα . . .
THΑ *iTHela*

Do you have . . . ?
Έχετε . . . ;
ehete

How much is this?
Πόσο κάνει αυτό;
poso kani afto

Where is the . . . department?
Που είναι το τμήμα των . . . ;
poo ine to tmima ton

Do you have any more of these?
Έχετε κι'άλλα απ'αυτά;
ehete kiala apafta

I'd like to change this, please
Θα ήθελα να το αλλάξω αυτό, παρακαλώ
THa íTHela na to alaxo afto, parakalo

Do you have anything less expensive?
Έχετε τίποτα φτηνότερο;
ehete tipota ftinotero

Do you have anything larger?
Έχετε κανένα μεγαλύτερο;
ehete kanena megalitero

Do you have anything smaller?
Έχετε κανένα μικρότερο;
ehete kanena mikrotero

Does it come in other colors?
Το έχετε σε άλλα χρώματα;
to ehete se ala hromata

Could you wrap it for me?
Μου το τυλίγετε;
moo to tiliyete

May I have a receipt?
Μου δίνετε μία απόδειξη;
moo thinete mia apothixi

May I have a bag, please?
Μου δίνετε μία σακούλα, παρακαλώ;
moo thinete mia sakoola, parakalo

Can I try it (them) on?
Μπορώ να το (τα) δοκιμάσω;
boro na to (ta) thokimaso

SHOPPING

Where do I pay?
Πού πληρώνω;
poo plir<u>o</u>no

I'm just looking
Απλώς κοιτάζω
apl<u>o</u>s kit<u>a</u>zo

I'll come back later
Θα επιστρέψω αργότερα
THa epistr<u>e</u>pso arg<u>o</u>tera

THINGS YOU'LL HEAR

Exipiret<u>i</u>ste?
Are you being helped?

<u>E</u>hete psil<u>a</u>?
Do you have anything smaller? (money)

Lip<u>a</u>me, mas tel<u>i</u>ose
I'm sorry, we're out of stock

Parakal<u>o</u> p<u>a</u>rte <u>e</u>na karots<u>a</u>ki/kal<u>a</u>THi
Please take a cart/basket

Aft<u>a</u> <u>e</u>hoome m<u>o</u>no
This is all we have

Then epistr<u>e</u>foome hr<u>i</u>mata
We cannot give cash refunds

THINGS YOU'LL SEE

αθλητικά	*aтнlitika*	sporting goods store
αλλαντικά	*alandika*	salami, sausages, ham, etc.
Αμερικανικό δολλάριο	*amerikaniko tholario*	US dollar
ανδρικά	*andrika*	menswear
ανθοπωλείο	*anтнopolio*	florist
αντίκες	*andikes*	antiques
αρτοποιείο	*artopi-io*	bakery
βιβλιοπωλείο	*vivliopolio*	bookstore
γλυκά	*glika*	cakes
γούνες	*goones*	furs
γραφείο ταξειδίων	*grafio taxithion*	travel agency
γυναικεία	*yinekia*	ladies' wear
δεν σιδερώνεται	*then sitheronete*	do not iron
δίσκοι, κασσέτες	*thiski, kasetes*	records, cassettes
δωδεκάδα	*thothekatha*	dozen
είδη γραφείου	*ithi grafioo*	office suppliers
είδη εξοχής	*ithi exohis*	holiday articles
ειδική προσφορά	*ithiki prosfora*	special offer
είσοδος ελευθέρα	*isothos elefтнera*	admission free
εκπτώσεις	*ekptosis*	sales
ευκαιρία	*efkeria*	bargain
εφημερίδες	*efimerithes*	newspapers
ζαχαροπλαστείο	*zaharoplastio*	pastry shop
ηλεκτρικά είδη	*ilektrika ithi*	electrical goods
ιχθυοπωλείο	*ihтнiopolio*	fish market
καλλυντικά	*kalindika*	perfume and cosmetics
κατεψυγμένα	*katepsigmena*	frozen food
καφές	*kafes*	coffee
κοσμηματοπωλείο	*kosmimatopolio*	jewelry
κρεατοπωλείο	*kreatopolio*	butcher
λαχανικά	*lahanika*	vegetables

→

μόδα	*motha*	fashion
παιδικά	*pethika*	children's wear
παιχνίδια	*pehnithia*	toys
παντοπωλείο	*pandopolio*	groceries
περιοδικά	*periothika*	magazines
ποιότητα	*piotita*	quality
ποτοπωλείο	*potopolio*	liquor store
ραφείο	*rafio*	tailor's
σελφ-σέρβις	"*self-service*"	self-service
σιδηρουργείο	*sithirooryio*	hardware store
τιμή	*timi*	price
τμήμα	*tmima*	department
το κιλό	*to kilo*	a kilo
τσάι	*tsai*	tea
υποδήματα	*ipothimata*	shoes
φρούτα	*froota*	fruit
φτηνό	*ftino*	inexpensive
φωτογραφείο	*fotografio*	camera store
χαλιά	*halia*	carpets
ψιλικά	*psilika*	small store

AT THE HAIRDRESSER'S

There are two types of hairdresser in Greece: the traditional ΚΟΥΡΕΙΟ (barbershop) which is only for men and where you can also have a shave, and the ΚΟΜΜΩΤΗΡΙΟ (hairdresser's) which is for both men and women. They are open Monday and Wednesday from 8 AM to 2 PM; Tuesday, Thursday, and Friday from 8 AM to 2 PM and then from 5 to 8.30 PM; and on Saturday from 8 AM to 4 PM.

USEFUL WORDS AND PHRASES

appointment	το ραντεβού	randevoo
beard	τα γένια	ta yenia
blond	ξανθιά	xanTHia
brush	η βούρτσα	i voortsa
comb	η τσατσάρα	i tsatsara
conditioner	το κοντίσιονερ	to "conditioner"
curlers	τα μπικουτί	ta bikooti
curly	σγουρά	sgoora
dark	μαύρα	mavra
gel	ο ζελές	o zeles
hair	τα μαλλιά	ta malia
haircut	το κούρεμα	to koorema
hairdresser	η κομμώτρια	i komotria
hair dryer	το πιστολάκι	to pistolaki
highlights	η μες	i mes
long	μακριά	makria
moustache	το μουστάκι	to moostaki
part	η χωρίστρα	i horistra
perm	η περμανάντ	i permanant
shampoo	το σαμπουάν	to sampooan
shave	το ξύρισμα	to xirisma
shaving cream	ο αφρός ξυρίσματος	o afros xirismatos
short	κοντά	konda
styling mousse	η μπριγιαντίνη	i briyandini
wavy	κυματιστά	kimatista

AT THE HAIRDRESSER'S

I'd like to make an appointment
Θα ήθελα να κλείσω ένα ραντεβού
THα ithela na kliso ena randevoo

Just a trim, please
Πάρτε τα μου λίγο, παρακαλώ
parteta moo ligo, parakalo

Not too much off
Μην κόψετε πολλά
mi kopsete pola

A bit more off here, please
Λίγο πιό πολύ εδώ, παρακαλώ
ligo pio poli etho, parakalo

I'd like a cut and blow-dry
Θα ήθελα ένα κούρεμα και χτένισμα
THα ithela ena koorema ke htenisma

I'd like a perm
Θα ήθελα μία περμανάντ
THα ithela mia permanant

I'd like highlights
Θα ήθελα ένα κάνο μες
THα ithela'na kano mes

THINGS YOU'LL SEE

ανδρικές κομμώσεις	*anthrikes komosis*	men's hairdresser
βαφή	*vafi*	hair dye
βάφω	*vafo*	to tint
ίσια	*isia*	straight
γυναικείες κομμώσεις	*yineki-e komosis*	ladies' salon
κόβω	*kovo*	to cut
κομμώσεις	*komosis*	hair stylist
κομμώτρια	*komotria*	hairdresser
κουρέας	*kooreas*	barber
κουρείο	*koorio*	barbershop
κούρεμα	*koorema*	haircut
λούσιμο	*loosimo*	wash
μαλλιά	*malia*	hair
μες	*mes*	highlights
μιζανπλί	*mizanpli*	set
ξύρισμα	*xirisma*	shave
περμανάντ	*permanant*	perm
ρολά	*rola*	curlers
σαμπουάν	*sampooan*	shampoo
σγουρά	*sgoora*	curly
στεγνώνω	*stegnono*	to dry
τα μπροστινά	*ta brostina*	the front
τα πλαϊνά	*ta plaina*	on the sides
τα πίσω	*ta piso*	at the back

SPORTS

Thanks to Greece's excellent climate, almost all outdoor sports are well catered to. Along the coasts of the mainland and on the islands, there are excellent opportunities for swimming, waterskiing, sailing, fishing (including underwater fishing), canoeing, and sailboarding. You will easily find someone to teach you waterskiing or windsurfing, and renting equipment generally poses no problem: everything from a beach umbrella to a sailboard is available at a reasonable charge.

If you want to discover the rarer beauties of Greece and the Archipelago, you must take to the sea. There are beautiful beaches, small islands, and sea caves accessible only by water. If you don't want to sail solo, there are several companies that will provide you with a captain—and a crew if you like. Detailed information is available from the Yacht Club of Greece, 18 Karageorgi Servias St., Munichia, Piraeus (tel: 417-9730).

In the mountainous areas such as the Pinthos range, Parnassos (near Delphi), Parnitha (just north of Athens), or Olympus, there is ample opportunity for walking and mountaineering. In the winter there is even skiing.

USEFUL WORDS AND PHRASES

athletics	ο αθλητισμός	o aтнlitismos
ball	η μπάλα	i bala
beach	η παραλία	i paralia
beach umbrella	η ομπρέλα του ήλιου	i obrela too ilioo
bicycle	το ποδήλατο	to pothilato
canoe	το κανώ	to kano
deck chair	η πολυθρόνα	i poliтнrona
diving board	η σανίδα	i sanitha
fishing	το ψάρεμα	to psarema
fishing rod	το καλάμι	to kalami
flippers	τα βατραχοπέδιλα	ta vatrahopethila
goggles	η μάσκα	i maska

golf	το γκολφ	to "golf"
golf course	το γήπεδο του γκολφ	to yipetho too "golf"
gymnastics	η γυμναστική	i yimnastiki
harpoon	το ψαροντούφεκο	to psarodoofeko
jogging	το τζόγκινγκ	to "jogging"
lake	η λίμνη	i limni
mountaineering	η ορειβασία	i orivasia
oxygen bottles	οι μπουκάλες οξυγόνου	i bookales oxigonoo
pedal boat	το ποδήλατο θαλάσσης	to pothilato THalasis
racket	η ρακέτα	i raketa
riding	η ιππασία	i ipasia
rowboat	η βάρκα με κουπιά	i varka me koopia
run (verb)	τρέχω	treho
sailboard	το γουίντ-σέρφινγκ	to "windsurfing"
sailing	η ιστιοπλοΐα	i istioplo-ia
sand	η άμμος	i amos
sea	η θάλασσα	i THalasa
skin diving	οι υποβρύχιες καταδύσεις	i ipovri-hies katathisis
snorkel	ο αναπνευστήρας	o anapnefstiras
soccer	το ποδόσφαιρο	to pothosfero
soccer match	ο ποδοσφαιρικός αγώνας	o pothosferikos agonas
stadium	το στάδιο	to stathio
swim (verb)	κολυμπώ	kolibo
swimming pool	η πισίνα	i pisina
tennis	το τέννις	to "tennis"
tennis court	το γήπεδο του τέννις	to yipetho too "tennis"
tennis racket	η ρακέτα	i raketa
tent	η σκηνή	i skini
underwater fishing	το υποβρύχιο ψάρεμα	to ipovrihio psarema

volleyball	το βόλλεϋ	to "volley"
walking	το περπάτημα	to perpatima
waterskiing	το θαλάσσιο σκι	to THalasio "ski"
water skis	τα πέδιλα του σκι	ta pethila too "ski"
wave (noun)	το κύμα	to kima
wet suit	η στολή	i stoli
	βατραχανθρώπου	vatrahanTHropou
yacht	το γιωτ	to "yacht"

How do I get to the beach?
Πως μπορώ να πάω στην παραλία;
pos boro na pao stin paralia

How deep is the water here?
Πόσο βαθύ είναι το νερό εδώ;
poso vaTHi ine to nero etho

Is there a swimming pool here?
Υπάρχει καμμία πισίνα εδώ;
iparhi kamia pisina etho

Is it safe to swim here?
Είναι ασφαλές το κολύμπι εδώ;
ine asfales to kolimbi etho

Can I fish here?
Μπορώ να ψαρέψω εδώ;
boro na psarepso etho

Do I need a license?
Χρειάζομαι δίπλωμα;
hriazome thiploma

How much does it cost per hour/day?
Πόσο στοιχίζει την ώρα/ημέρα;
poso sti-hizi tin ora/imera

Am I allowed to camp here?
Επιτρέπεται να κατασκηνώσω εδώ;
epitrepete na kataskinoso etho

I would like to take waterskiing lessons
Θα ήθελα να πάρω μαθήματα σκι
ΤΗΑ *ithela na paro maThimata "ski"*

Where can I rent . . . ?
Που μπορώ να νοικιάσω . . . ;
poo boro na nikiaso

THINGS YOU'LL SEE OR HEAR

αθλητικές εγκαταστάσεις	*aTHlitikes egatastasis*	sports facilities
αθλητικό κέντρο	*aTHlitiko kendro*	sports center
ακτή	*akti*	beach
άλσος	*alsos*	wooded park
απαγορεύεται η κατασκήνωση	*apagorevete i kataskinosi*	no camping
απαγορεύεται η κολύμβηση	*apagorevete i kolimvisi*	no swimming
απαγορεύεται το ψάρεμα	*apagorevete to psarema*	no fishing
απαγορευμένη περιοχή	*apagorevmeni periohi*	restricted area
απαγορεύονται οι καταδύσεις	*apagorevonde i katathisis*	no diving
γήπεδο	*yipetho*	soccer field
γήπεδο τέννις	*yipetho "tennis"*	tennis court
εισιτήρια	*isitiria*	tickets
ενοικιάζονται	*enikiazonde*	for rent
θαλάσσια σπορ	*THalasia spor*	water sports

→

ιππόδρομος	*ipothromos*	racecourse (for horses)
ιστιοφόρο	*istioforo*	sailboat
κωπηλατώ	*kopilato*	to row
λιμενική Αστυνομία	*limeniki astinomia*	harbor police
λιμήν	*limin*	port
μαρίνα	*marina*	marina
μαθήματα σκι	*maTHimata "ski"*	waterskiing lessons
πρώτες βοήθειες	*protes voiTHies*	first aid
ποδήλατα	*pothilata*	bicycles
στάδιο	*stathio*	stadium
χώρος διά ποδηλάτες	*horos ia pothilates*	bicycle path

POST OFFICES AND BANKS

Post offices in Greece only deal with mail, so don't expect to find telephones there. (If you want to make a phone call, use a telephone booth or go to the telephone exchange—OTE). Also, if you want to send a telegram or a fax, you'll have to go to the OTE and not to a post office. Stamps can be bought in post offices, but many Greeks go to street kiosks where you can also buy postcards. Mailboxes are yellow in Greece. Mail can be sent to you, marked poste-restante, for collection at the post office of any town. Don't forget that you won't be able to collect your mail unless you have your passport with you.

All banks are open from 8 AM to 2 PM Monday to Thursday, and 8 AM to 1:30 PM on Friday. In larger towns and resorts, at least one bank will reopen briefly for currency exchange in the evening and on Saturday mornings during the summer season. Banks close for public holidays and sometimes for local festivals. ATMs are found in major towns and resorts, but seldom elsewhere.

The Greek unit of currency is the **drachma** (Dr). The best exchange rates for currency, traveler's checks, and Eurochecks are found in banks and post offices, although you can also change money in travel agencies, hotels, tourist offices, and car rental agencies. Some large towns also have electronic currency exchange machines.

Credit cards are not generally accepted at inexpensive restaurants and stores, but they are useful at most hotels and for large purchases. They can also be used to obtain cash advances in some banks (with a 15,000 Dr minimum withdrawal) and from ATMs. Be advised of a processing charge for such transactions.

Useful Words and Phrases

airmail	αεροπορικώς	*aeroporikos*
ATM	το μηχάνημα ανάληψης μετρητών	*to mihanima analipsis metriton*
bank	η τράπεζα	*i trapeza*
bill *(money)*	το χαρτονόμισμα	*to hartonomisma*
cash	τα μετρητά	*ta metrita*
change *(noun)*	το συνάλλαγμα	*to sinalagma*
(verb)	αλλάζω συνάλλαγμα	*allazo sinalagma*
check	η επιταγή	*i epitayi*
checkbook	το βιβλιάριο επιταγών	*to vivliario epitagon*
coins	κέρματα	*kermata*
counter	το ταμείο	*to tamio*
credit card	η πιστωτική κάρτα	*i pistotiki karta*
customs form	τελωνιακή δήλωση	*teloniaki thilosi*
delivery	η διανομή	*i thianomi*
deposit *(noun)*	η κατάθεση	*kataTHesi*
(verb)	καταθέτω	*kataTHeto*
exchange rate	η συναλλαγματική ισοτιμία	*i sinalagmatiki isotimia*
form	η αίτηση	*i etisi*
international money order	η διεθνής τραπεζική εντολή πληρωμής	*i thieTHnis trapeziki endoli pliromis*
letter	το γράμμα	*to grama*
mail	το ταχυδρομείο	*to tahithromio*
mailbox	το γραμματοκιβώτιο	*to gramatokivotio*
mailman	ο ταχυδρόμος	*o tahithromos*
money order	η ταχυδρομική επιταγή	*i tahithromiki epitayi*
package/parcel	το δέμα	*to thema*
post	το ταχυδρομείο	*to tahithromio*
postage rates	τα ταχυδρομικά έξοδα	*ta tahithromika exotha*

postal order	η ταχυδρομική επιταγή	i tahithromiki epitayi
postcard	η κάρτα	i karta
poste-restante	το ποστ-ρεστάντ	to post-restant
post office	το ταχυδρομείο	to tahithromio
registered letter	το συστημένο γράμμα	to sistimeno grama
stamp	το γραμματόσημο	to gramatosimo
telegram	το τηλεγράφημα	to tilegrafima
traveler's check	η ταξιδιωτική επιταγή	i taxithiotiki epitayi
US dollar	το Αμερικανικό δολλάριο	amerikaniko tholario
withdraw	κάνω ανάληψη	kano analipsi
withdrawal	η ανάληψη	i analipsi
zip code, postal code	ο ταχυδρομικός τομέας	o tahithromikos tomeas

How much is a letter/postcard to . . . ?
Πόσο κάνει το γραμματόσημο για ένα γράμμα/μία κάρτα για . . . ;
poso kani to gramatosimo ya ena grama/mia karta ya

I would like three 27-drachma stamps
Θα ήθελα τρία γραμματόσημα των είκοσι επτά δραχμών
THa itHela tria gramatosima ton ikosi epta thrahmon

I want to register this letter
Θέλω να στείλω αυτό το γράμμα συστημένο
THelo na stilo afto to grama sistimeno

I want to send this package to . . .
Θέλω να στείλω αυτό το δέμα στην . . .
THelo na stilo afto to thema stin

85

How long does the mail to . . . take?
Πόσο κάνει να φτάσει στην . . . ;
poso kani na ftasi stin

Where can I mail this?
Που μπορώ να ταχυδρομήσω αυτό;
poo boro na tahithromiso afto

Is there any mail for me?
Υπάρχει κανένα γράμμα για μένα;
iparhi kanena grama ya mena?

I'd like to send a telegram
Θα ήθελα να στείλω ένα τηλεγράφημα
τηα itHela na stilo ena tilegrafima

This is to go airmail
Αυτό να πάει αεροπορικώς
afto na pai aeroporikos

I'd like to change this into 1000-drachma bills
Θα ήθελα να το αλλάξω αυτό σε χαρτονομίσματα των
χίλια δραχμών
τηα itHela na to alaxo afto se hartonomismata ton hilia thrahmon

Can I cash these traveler's checks?
Μπορώ να εξαργυρώσω αυτές τις ταξιδιωτικές επιταγές;
boro na exargyroso aftes tis taxithiotikes epitayes

What is the exchange rate for the dollar?
Ποιά είναι η τιμή συναλλάγματος για του δολλάριο;
pia ine i timi sinalagmatos yia tu tholario

Can I draw cash using this credit card?
Μπορώ να πάρω μετρητά με αυτή την πιστωτική κάρτα;
boro na paro metrita me afti tin pistotiki karta

Could you give me smaller notes?
Μπορείτε να μου δώσετε μικρότερα χαρτονομίσματα;
borite na moo thosete mikrotera hartonomismata

THINGS YOU'LL SEE

αεροπορικώς	*aeroporikos*	by airmail
αλλαγή συναλλάγματος	*allayi sinalagmatos*	cash dispenser
αναλήψεις	*analipsis*	withdrawals
ανοικτά	*anikta*	open
αποστολέας	*apostoleas*	sender
γραμματοκιβώτιο	*gramatokivotio*	mailbox
γραμματόσημο	*gramatosima*	stamps
δέματα	*themata*	packages, parcels
διεύθυνση	*thi-efthinsi*	address
ΕΛΤΑ	*elta*	Greek Post Office
εξωτερικού	*exoterikoo*	postage abroad
επιστολές	*epistoles*	letters
εσωτερικό	*esoterikoo*	domestic postage
καρτ-ποστάλ	*kart-postal*	postcard
καταθέσεις	*kataTHesis*	deposits
κατεπείγον	*katepigon*	express
κλειστά	*klista*	closed
μηχάνημα ανάληψης μετρητών	*mihanima analipsis metriton*	ATM
ξένο νόμισμα	*xeno nomisma*	foreign currency
ποστ-ρεστάντ	*post restant*	poste restante
συνάλλαγμα	*sinalagma*	exchange
συστημένα	*sistimena*	registered mail
ταμείο	*tamio*	cash desk
ταμίας	*tamias*	cashier
ταχυδρομείο	*tahithromio*	post office
ταχυδρομικός τομεύς	*tahithromikos tomefs*	zip code, postal code

→

τηλεγραφήμματα	*tilegrafimata*	telegrams
τιμές συναλλάγματος	*times sinalagmatos*	exchange rates
τράπεζα	*trapeza*	bank
τραπεζικές εντολές πληρωμής	*trapezikes endoles pliromis*	money orders
τρέχοντες λογαριασμοί	*trehondes logariasmi*	current accounts
ώρες λειτουργίας	*ores litooryias*	opening hours

TELEPHONES

Telephones and telegrams are the responsibility of the OTE (Telecommunications Organization of Greece), not of the post office. The public phone booths are blue for local calls and orange for long distance.

Don't forget that the little Greek "kiosks" where you can buy cigarettes, postcards, etc., also have a telephone for public use. There are also pay phones in cafeterias and restaurants but, if you want to make a call home or a long-distance call within Greece, it is best to go to an OTE. There you will be given a booth and asked to pay at the desk when you have finished your call.

The tones you'll hear when making a call in Greece are:

Dial tone:	same as in US
Ringing:	repeated long tone
Busy signal:	rapid beeps

The dialing code for the US is 001.

Useful telephone numbers:

Medical care	166
Police	100
Tourist Police	171
Fire	199
Roadside assistance	104

USEFUL WORDS AND PHRASES

call (*noun*)	το τηλεφώνημα	to tilefonima
(*verb*)	τηλεφωνήσω	tilefoniso
code	ο κωδικός	o kothikos
collect call	το τηλεφώνημα κολέκτ	to tilefonima kolekt
crossed line	η μπλεγμένη γραμμή	i blegmeni grami
dial (*verb*)	καλώ	kalo
directory inquiries	οι πληροφορίες	i plirofories
emergency	η επείγουσα ανάγκη	i epigoosa anagi
extension	το εσωτερικό	to esoteriko
international call	το υπεραστικό	to iperastiko
number	ο αριθμός	o ariTHmos
pay phone	το τηλέφωνο με κέρματα	to tilefono me kermata
receiver	το ακουστικό	to akoostiko
telephone	το τηλέφωνο	to tilefono
telephone booth	ο τηλεφωνικός θάλαμος	o tilefonikos THalamos
telephone directory	ο τηλεφωνικός κατάλογος	tilefonikos katalogos
wrong number	λάθος νούμερο	laTHos noomero

Where is the nearest phone booth?
Που είναι ο πλησιέστερος τηλεφωνικός θάλαμος;
poo ine o plisi-esteros tilefonikos THalamos

Hello, this is . . . speaking
Χαίρετε, είμαι ο . . .
herete, ime o

Is that . . . ?
Ο/η . . . ;
o/i

Speaking
ο ίδιος
o ithios

I would like to speak to . . .
Θα ήθελα να μιλήσω στον . . .
THa iTHela na miliso ston

Extension . . . , please
Εσωτερικό . . . παρακαλώ
esoteriko . . . parakalo

Please tell him . . . called
Παρακαλώ του λέτε ότι τηλεφώνησε ο/η . . .
parakalo too lete oti tilefonise o/i

Ask him to call me back, please
Πέστε του να με ξαναπάρει παρακαλώ
peste too na me xanapari parakalo

My number is . . .
το τηλέφωνό μου είναι . . .
to tilefono moo ine

Do you know where he is?
Ξέρετε που είναι;
xerete poo ine

When will he be back?
Πότε θα επιστρέψει;
pote THa epistrepsi

Could you leave him a message?
Μπορείτε να του αφήσετε ένα μήνυμα;
borite na too afisete ena minimas

THINGS YOU'LL HEAR

O ithios
Speaking

Lipame, then ine etho
Sorry, he's not in

Pios tilefoni?
Who's calling?

Me pion THelete na milisete?
Whom would you like to speak to?

Bori na sas pari piso?
Can he call you back?

Pio ine to tilefono sas?
What's your number?

Pirate lathos noomero
You've got the wrong number

THa epistrepsi stis . . .
He'll be back at . . .

THa sas sintheso
I'll put you through

I'll call back later
Θα σε ξαναπάρω αργότερα
THA se xanapa̱ro argo̱tera

Sorry, wrong number
Πήρατε λάθος αριθμό
pi̱rate la̱THos ariTHmo̱

Is there a telephone directory?
Υπάρχει κανένας τηλεφωνικός κατάλογος;
ipa̱rhi kane̱nas tilefoniko̱s kata̱logos

I would like the directory for . . .
Θα ήθελα τον κατάλογο για . . .
THA i̱THela ton kata̱logo ya

Can I call abroad from here?
Μπορώ να τηλεφωνήσω στο εξωτερικό από εδώ;
boro̱ na tilefoni̱so sto exoteriko̱ apo̱ etho̱

How much is a call to . . . ?
Πόσο στοιχίζει ένα τηλεφώνημα στο . . . ;
po̱so sti-hi̱zi e̱na tilefo̱nima sto

I would like to make a collect call
Θα ήθελα τα έξοδα να πληρωθούν εκεί
THA i̱THela ta e̱xotha na pliroTHo̱on eki̱

I would like a number in . . .
Θέλω ένα αριθμό στην . . .
THe̱lo e̱na ariTHmo̱ stin

THINGS YOU'LL SEE OR HEAR

ακουστικό	*akoostiko*	receiver
άμεσος δράσις	*amesos thrasis*	emergencies, police
αριθμός	*ariᴛʜmos*	number
δεν λειτουργεί	*then litooryi*	out of order
καλεί	*kali*	ringing
καλέσατε	*kalesate*	dial
κέρματα	*kermata*	coins
κωδικός	*kothikos*	code
λάθος νούμερο	*laᴛʜos noomero*	wrong number
μιλάει	*milai*	busy
μονάδες	*monathes*	units
νούμερο	*noomero*	number
ΟΤΕ	*ote*	telephone
πυροσβεστική	*pirosvestiki*	fire department
σηκώσατε	*sikosate*	pick up
τηλεγραφήματα	*tilegrafimata*	telegrams
τηλεφώνημα	*tilefonima*	call
τηλεφωνικός θάλαμος	*tilefonikos ᴛʜalamos*	telephone booth
τηλεφωνικός κατάλογος	*tilefonikos katalogos*	telephone directory
τηλέφωνο	*tilefono*	telephone
τηλεφωνώ	*tilefono*	to call
τοπικό	*topiko*	local call
φωτιά	*fotia*	fire
χαίρετε	*herete*	hello
χρυσός οδηγός	*hrisos othigos*	yellow pages
υπεραστικό	*iperastiko*	long-distance call, international call

HEALTH

If you get sick or have an accident in Greece—nothing too
serious—you can always go to a pharmacist, who is usually
qualified to treat minor injuries. Pharmacies (*to farmakio*) are
identified by a red cross, and all towns have one that is open
all night on a rotation system. Look for a sign on the door
that will tell you which is the drugstore on duty.

USEFUL WORDS AND PHRASES

accident	το ατύχημα	*to atihima*
ambulance	το ασθενοφόρο	*to asthenoforo*
anemic	αναιμικός	*anemikos*
appendicitis	η σκωληκοειδίτις	*i skoliko-ithitis*
appendix	η σκωληκοειδής απόφυση	*i skoliko-ithis apofisi*
aspirin	η ασπιρίνη	*i aspirini*
asthma	το άσθμα	*to asthma*
backache	ο πόνος στη πλάτη	*o ponos sti plati*
bandage	ο επίδεσμος	*o epithesmos*
(*adhesive*)	ο γύψος	*o yipsos*
bite	το δάγκωμα	*to thagoma*
(*by insect*)	το τσίμπημα	*to tssbima*
bladder	η κύστη	*i kisti*
blister	η φουσκάλα	*i fooskala*
blood	το αίμα	*to ema*
blood donor	ο αιμοδότης	*o emothotis*
burn	το κάψιμο	*o kapsimo*
cancer	ο καρκίνος	*o karkinos*
chest	το στήθος	*to stithos*
chicken pox	η ανεμοβλογιά	*i anemovloya*
cold	το κρυολόγημα	*to krioloyima*
concussion	η διάσειση	*i thiasisi*
constipation	η δυσκοιλιότητα	*i thiskiliotita*

contact lenses	οι φακοί επαφής	i faki epafis
corn	ο κάλος	o kalos
cough	ο βήχας	o vihas
cut	το κόψιμο	to kopsimo
dentist	ο οδοντίατρος	o othondiatros
diabetes	το ζάχαρο	to zaharo
diarrhea	η διάρροια	i thiaria
dizzy	ζαλισμένος	zalismenos
doctor	ο γιατρός	o yatros
drugstore	ο φαρμακοποιός	o farmakopios
earache	ο πόνος στ'αυτί	o ponos st'afti
fever	ο πυρετός	o piretos
filling	το σφράγισμα	to sfrayisma
first aid	οι πρώτες βοήθειες	i protes voiTHies
flu	η γρίππη	i gripi
fracture	το κάταγμα	to katagma
German measles	η ερυθρά	i eriTHra
glasses	τα γυαλιά	ta yalia
hay fever	ο πυρετός	o piretos
	του χόρτου	too hortoo
headache	ο πονοκέφαλος	o ponokefalos
heart	η καρδιά	i karthia
heart attack	η καρδιακή	i karthiaki
	προσβολή	prosvoli
hemorrhage	η αιμοραγία	i emorayia
hospital	το νοσοκομείο	to nosokomio
ill	άρρωστος	arostos
indigestion	η δυσπεψία	i thispepsia
injection	η ένεση	i enesi
itch	η φαγούρα	i fagoora
kidney	το νεφρό	to nefro
lump	ο όγκος	o ogos
measles	η ιλαρά	i ilara
migraine	η ημικρανία	i imikrania

motion sickness	η ναυτία	i naftia
mumps	οι μαγουλάδες	i magoolathes
nausea	η ναυτία	i naftia
nurse	η νοσοκόμα	i nosokoma
operation	η εγχείρηση	i enhirisi
optician	ο οπτικός	o optikos
pain	ο πόνος	o ponos
penicillin	η πενικιλλίνη	i penikilini
pneumonia	η πνευμονία	i pnevmonia
pregnant	έγκυος	egios
prescription	η συνταγή	i sindayi
rheumatism	οι ρευματισμοί	i revmatismi
scald	το έγκαυμα	to egavma
scratch	η γρατζουνιά	i grazoonia
smallpox	η ευλογιά	i evloya
splinter	η αγκίδα	i agitha
sprain	το διάστρεμμα	to thiastrema
sting	το τσούξιμο	to tsooximo
stomach	το στομάχι	to stomahi
temperature	ο πυρετός	o piretos
tonsils	οι αμυγδαλές	i amigthales
toothache	ο πονόδοντος	o ponothondos
ulcer	το έλκος	to elkos
vaccination	ο εμβολιασμός	o emvoliasmos
vomit (verb)	κάνω εμετό	kano emeto
whooping cough	ο κοκκύτης	o kokitis

I have a pain in . . .
Έχω ένα πόνο στο . . .
eho ena pono sto

I do not feel well
Δεν αισθάνομαι καλά
then esTHanome kala

I feel faint
Μου έρχετε λιποθυμία
moo erhete lipoτΗimia

I feel sick
Θα κάνω εμετό
τΗa kano emets

I feel dizzy
Ζαλίζομαι
zalizome

I have a sore throat
Πονάει ο λαιμός μου
ponai o lemos moo

It hurts here
Πονάει εδώ
ponai etho

It's a sharp pain
Είναι δυνατός πόνος
ine thinatos o ponos

It's a dull pain
Έχω ένα μικρό πόνο
eho ena mikro pono

It hurts all the time
Πονάει συνέχεια
ponai sinehia

It only hurts now and then
Με πονάει πότε-πότε
me ponai pote-pote

It hurts when you touch it
Με πονάει όταν το ακουμπάς
me ponai otan to akoobas

It hurts more at night
Πονάει περισσότερο την νύχτα
ponai perisotero ti nihta

It stings
Τσούζει
tsoozi

It aches
Πονάει
ponai

I have a temperature
Έχω πυρετό
eho pireto

I need a prescription for . . .
Χρειάζομαι συνταγή για . . .
hriazome sidayi ya

I normally take . . .
Συνήθως παίρνω . . .
sinithos perno

I'm allergic to . . .
Είμαι αλλεργικός με . . .
ime aleryikos me

Have you got anything for . . . ?
Έχετε τίποτα για . . . ;
ehete tipota ya

Do I need a prescription for . . . ?
Χρειάζομαι συνταγή για . . . ;
hriazome sindayi ya

I have lost a filling
Μου έφυγε ένα σφράγισμα
moo efiye ena sfrayisma

THINGS YOU'LL HEAR

Na pernis . . . hapia/thiskia tin imera
Take . . . pills/tablets per day

Me nero
With water

Na ta masate
Chew them

Mia fora/thio fores/tris fores tin imera
Once/twice/three times a day

Mono otan pas ya ipno
Only when you go to bed

Ti pernis siniTHos?
What do you normally take?

Prepi na this ena yatro?
I think you should see a doctor

Lipame, then to ehoome
I'm sorry, we don't have that

Hriazese sindayi yafto
For that you need a prescription

THINGS YOU'LL SEE

αίθουσα αναμονής	_eтHoosa anamonis_	waiting room
ακτίνες-Χ	_aktines hi_	X-rays
ασθενοφόρο	_asтHenoforo_	ambulance
αφροδισιολόγος	_afrothisiologos_	venereal disease specialist
γιατρός	_yatros_	doctor
γυαλιά	_yalia_	glasses
γυναικολόγος	_yinekologos_	gynecologist
δερματολόγος	_thermatologos_	dermatologist
διανυκτερεύον	_thianiktereyon_	open all night
ειδικός	_ithikos_	specialist
εξετάσεις	_exetasis_	checkup
ησυχία	_isihia_	quiet
ιατρείο	_iatrio_	doctor's office
ιατρός	_iatros_	doctor
κλινική	_kliniki_	clinic
νοσοκόμα	_nosokoma_	nurse
νοσοκομείο	_nosokomio_	hospital
οδοντιατρός	_othondiatros_	dentist
οδοντιατρείο	_othondiatrio_	dentist's
ούλο	_oolo_	gum
οπτικός	_optikos_	optician
παθολόγος	_paтHologos_	General Practitioner
παιδίατρος	_pethiatros_	pediatrician
πίεση αίματος	_pi-esi ematos_	blood pressure
πρώτες βοήθειες	_protes voiтHi-es_	first aid
σφράγισμα	_sfrayisma_	filling
τοπική αναισθησία	_topiki anesтHisia_	local anesthetic
φαρμακείο	_farmakio_	drugstore
φαρμακοποιός	_farmakopios_	pharmacist
ειρουργείο	_hirooryio_	operating room
ώρες επισκέψεως	_ores episkepseos_	visiting hours

CONVERSION TABLES

Distances

Distances are marked in kilometers. To convert kilometers to miles, divide the km by 8 and multiply by 5 (1 km being five-eighths of a mile). Convert miles to km by dividing the miles by 5 and multiplying by 8. A mile is 1609 m (1.609 km).

km	miles *or* km	miles
1.61	1	0.62
3.22	2	1.24
4.83	3	1.86
6.44	4	2.48
8.05	5	3.11
9.66	6	3.73
11.27	7	4.35
12.88	8	4.97
14.49	9	5.59
16.10	10	6.21

Other units of length:

1 centimeter	= 0.39 in	1 inch	= 25.4 millimeters
1 meter	= 39.37 in	1 foot	= 0.30 meter (30 cm)
10 meters	= 32.81 ft	1 yard	= 0.91 meter

Weights

The unit you will come into most contact with is the kilogram (kilo), equivalent to 2 lb 3oz. To convert kg to lbs, multiply by 2 and add one-tenth of the result (thus, 6 kg x 2 = 12 + 1.2, or 13.2 lbs). One ounce is about 28 grams, and 1 lb is 454 g.

grams	ounces	ounces	grams
50	1.76	1	28.3
100	3.53	2	56.7
250	8.81	4	113.4
500	17.63	8	226.8

kg	lbs *or* kg	lbs
0.45	1	2.20
0.91	2	4.41
1.36	3	6.61
1.81	4	8.82
2.27	5	11.02
2.72	6	13.23
3.17	7	15.43
3.63	8	17.64
4.08	9	19.84
4.53	10	22.04

TEMPERATURE

To convert centigrade or Celsius degrees into Fahrenheit, the accurate method is to multiply the C° figure by 1.8 and add 32. Similarly, to convert F° to C°, subtract 32 from the F° figure and divide by 1.8. This will give you a truly accurate conversion, but it takes a little time in mental arithmetic! See the table below:

C°	F°	C°	F°	
-10	14	25	77	
0	32	30	86	
5	41	36.9	98.6	*body temperature*
10	50	40	104	
20	68	100	212	*boiling point*

LIQUIDS

One "imperial" gallon is roughly 4.5 liters, but American drivers must remember that the US gallon is only 3.8 liters (1 liter = 1.06 US quart). In the following table, US gallons are used:

liters	gals or l	gals
3.77	1	0.27
7.54	2	0.53
11.31	3	0.80
15.08	4	1.06
18.85	5	1.33
22.62	6	1.59
26.39	7	1.86
30.16	8	2.12
33.93	9	2.37
37.70	10	2.65
75.40	20	5.31
113.10	30	7.96
150.80	40	10.61
188.50	50	13.26

TIRE PRESSURES

lb/sq in	15	18	20	22	24
kg/sq cm	1.1	1.3	1.4	1.5	1.7

lb/sq in	26	28	30	33	35
kg/sq cm	1.8	2.0	2.1	2.3	2.5

MINI-DICTIONARY

about: about 16 perįpoo thekaexi
accelerator to gazi
accident to thistįhima
accommodations thomatia
ache o ponos
adaptor *(electrical)* to polaplo
address i thiefɾHinsi
adhesive i kola
after meta
aftershave i kolonia meta to
  xirįsma
again xana
against enandion
air-conditioning o klimatismos
aircraft to aeroplano
air freshener to aposmitiko horoo
airline i aerogrami
airport to aerothromio
Albania i Alvania
Albanian *(man)* o Alvanos
  (woman) i Alvani
  (adj.) Alvanikos
alcohol to alko-ol
all ola
  all the streets oli i thromi
  that's all, thanks tįpota alo,
  efharisto
almost s-hethon
alone monos
already įthi
always panda
am: I am įme
ambulance to asTHenoforo
America i Amerikį
American *(man)* o Amerikanos
  (woman) i Amerikana
  (adj.) Amerikanikos
and ke

ankle o astragalos
anorak to boofan
another *(room)* alo
  (coffee) kialo
antifreeze to andipsiktiko
antiques shop to paleopolio
antiseptic to andisiptiko
apartment to thiamerisma
aperitif to aperitif
appendicitis i skolikoithitis
appetite i orexi
apple to milo
application form i etisi
appointment to radevoo
apricot to verikoko
are: you are įse
  we are įmaste
  they are įne
arm to heri
art i tehni
art gallery i pinakoтНiki
artist o kalitehnis
as: as soon as possible oso pio
  grigora yinete
ashtray to stahtothohio
asleep: he's asleep kimate
aspirin i aspirini
at: at the post office sto tahithromio
  at night ti nihta
  at 3 o'clock stis tris i ora
Athens i AтHina
ATM to mihanima analipsis
attractive elkistikos
aunt i thia
Australia i Afstralia
Australian *(man)* o Afstralos
  (woman) i Afstraleza
  (adj.) Afstralezikos

Austria i Afstria
Austrian *(man)* o Afstriakos
  (woman) i Afstriaki
  (adj.) Afstriakos
automatic aftomatos
away: is it far away? ine makria?
  go away! fiye!
awful apesios
ax to tsekoori
axle o axonas

baby to moro
baby carriage to karotsaki
back *(not front)* piso
  (body) i plati
backpack to sakithio
bacon to beikon
  bacon and eggs avga me beikon
bad kakos
baggage i aposkeves
baggage rack i skara
baggage room o horos filaxis
  aposkevon
bait to tholoma
bake psino
baker o foornaris
balcony to balkoni
ball *(soccer)* i bala
  (tennis) to balaki
  (dance) i horosperitha
ballpoint pen o markathoros
banana i banana
band *(musicians)* to sigrotima
bandage o epithesmos
  (adhesive) o lefkoplastis
bank i trapeza
banknote to hartonomisma
bar to bar
  bar of chocolate i sokolata
barbecue to psisimo stin exohi
barbershop to koorio

bargain i efkeria
basement to ipoyio
basket to kalaTHi
bath to banio
  to have a bath kano banio
bathing cap o skoofos too banioo
bathing suit to mayio
bathroom to banio
battery i bataria
beach i paralia
beans ta fasolia
beard ta yenia
because epithi
bed to krevati
bed linen ta sendonia
bedroom to ipnothomatio
beef to mos-hari
beer i bira
before prin
beginner o arharios
behind apo piso
beige bez
Belgian *(man)* o Velgos
  (woman) i Velyitha
  (adj.) Velyikos
Belgium to Velyio
bell *(church)* i kabana
  (door) to koothooni
below apo kato
belt i zoni
beside thipla apo
best aristos
better kaliteros
between metaxi
bicycle to pothilato
big megalos
bikini to bikini
bill o logariasmos
bird to pooli
birthday ta yeneTHlia
  happy birthday! hronia pola!
birthday present to thoro ton
  yeneTHlion

bite *(verb)* thag<u>o</u>no
  (noun) i thagoni<u>a</u>
  (by insect) to tsibima
bitter pikr<u>o</u>s
black m<u>a</u>vros
blackberry to m<u>oo</u>ro
blanket i koov<u>e</u>rta
bleach *(verb: hair)* xaspr<u>i</u>zo
  (noun) i hlor<u>i</u>ni
blind *(cannot see)* o tifl<u>o</u>s
blister i foosk<u>a</u>la
blood to <u>e</u>ma
blouse i bl<u>oo</u>za
blue ble
boat to pl<u>i</u>o
  (smaller) to k<u>a</u>iki
body to s<u>o</u>ma
boil vr<u>a</u>zo
bolt *(verb)* sirt<u>o</u>no
  (noun: on door) o s<u>i</u>rtis
bone to k<u>o</u>kalo
book *(noun)* to vivl<u>i</u>o
  (verb) kl<u>i</u>no
bookstore to vivliop<u>o</u>lio
boot i b<u>o</u>ta
border ta s<u>i</u>nora
boring var<u>e</u>t<u>o</u>s
born: I was born in . . .
  yen<u>i</u>THika stin . . .
both ke i th<u>i</u>o
  both of them i th<u>i</u>o toos
  both of us i th<u>i</u>o mas
  both . . . and . . . ke . . . ke . . .
bottle to book<u>a</u>li
bottle-opener to aniht<u>i</u>ri
bottom o p<u>a</u>tos
  (sea) o v<u>i</u>TH<u>o</u>s
bowl to bol
box to koot<u>i</u>
boy to ag<u>o</u>ri
boyfriend o f<u>i</u>los
bra to soutien
bracelet to vrahi<u>o</u>li

braces i tir<u>a</u>ndes
brake *(noun)* to fr<u>e</u>no
  (verb) fren<u>a</u>ro
brandy to koni<u>a</u>k
bread to psom<u>i</u>
breakdown *(car)* i mihanik<u>i</u> vl<u>a</u>vi
  (nervous) o nevrik<u>o</u>s klonism<u>o</u>s
breakfast to proin<u>o</u>
breathe anapn<u>e</u>o
  I can't breathe then bor<u>o</u> na
  anapn<u>e</u>fso
bridge i y<u>e</u>fira
briefcase o hartof<u>i</u>lakas
British Vretanik<u>o</u>s
brochure to thiafimistik<u>o</u>
broken spasm<u>e</u>no
  broken leg to spasm<u>e</u>no p<u>o</u>thi
brooch i karf<u>i</u>tsa
brother o athelf<u>o</u>s
brown kaf<u>e</u>s
bruise i melani<u>a</u>
brush *(noun)* i v<u>oo</u>rtsa
  (paint) to pin<u>e</u>lo
  (verb) voorts<u>i</u>zo
bucket o koov<u>a</u>s
building to kt<u>i</u>rio
Bulgaria i V<u>oo</u>lgaria
Bulgarian *(man)* o V<u>oo</u>lgaros
  (woman) i V<u>oo</u>lgara
  (adj.) Voolgarik<u>o</u>s
bumper o profilaht<u>i</u>ras
burglar o thiar<u>i</u>ktis
burn *(verb)* k<u>e</u>o
  (noun) to k<u>a</u>psimo
bus to leofor<u>i</u>o
  (long-distance) to p<u>oo</u>lman
bus station o staTHm<u>o</u>s leofor<u>i</u>on
  (long-distance) o staTHm<u>o</u>s
  iperastik<u>o</u>n leofor<u>i</u>on
business i thooli<u>e</u>s
  it's none of your business
  then se afor<u>a</u>

busy *(occupied)* katilim_e_nos
  (crowded) polisihnastos
but al_a_
butcher o hasapis
butter to v_oo_tiro
button to koob_i_
buy agor_a_zo
by: by the window kond_a_ sto par_a_THiro
  by Friday _e_os tin paraskev_i_
  by myself m_o_nos moo

cabbage to l_a_hano
cable car to telefer_i_k
café i kafet_e_ria
cake i "cake"
calculator to kompiooter_a_ki
call: what's it called?
  pos to l_e_ne?
camera i fotografik_i_ mihan_i_
camper to troh_o_spito
campsite to "camping"
camshaft o str_o_falos
can *(tin)* i kons_e_rva
  can I have . . . ? bor_o_ na _e_ho . . . ?
Canada o Kanath_a_s
Canadian *(man)* o Kanath_o_s
  (woman) i Kanath_e_za
  (adj.) Kanath_e_zikos
cancer o kark_i_nos
candle to ker_i_
candy i karam_e_la
canoe to kan_o_
can opener to aniht_i_ri
cap *(bottle)* to kap_a_ki
  (hat) o sk_oo_fos
car to aftok_i_nito
carbonated me anTHrakik_o_
carburetor to karbirat_e_r
card i k_a_rta
cardigan i zak_e_ta
careful prosektik_o_s
  be careful! pros_e_he!

carpet to hal_i_
carriage *(train)* to vag_o_ni
carrot to kar_o_to
case i val_i_tsa
cash ta metrit_a_
  (coins) ta psil_a_
  to pay cash plir_o_no metrit_i_s
cassette i kas_e_ta
cassette player to kaset_o_fono
castle to k_a_stro
cat i g_a_ta
cathedral o kaTHethrik_o_s na_o_s
cauliflower to koonoop_i_thi
cave i spili_a_
cemetery to nekrotaf_i_o
center to k_e_ndro
certificate i _a_thia
chair i kar_e_kla
chamber music i moosik_i_ thomat_i_oo
chambermaid i kamari_e_ra
change *(noun: money)* ta r_e_sta
  (verb: clothes) al_a_zo
cheers! *(toast)* is iyi_a_n!
cheese to tir_i_
check i epitay_i_
checkbook to karn_e_ ton
  epitag_o_n
cherry to ker_a_si
chess to sk_a_ki
chest to st_i_THos
chewing gum i ts_i_hla
chicken to kot_o_poolo
child to peth_i_
children ta pethi_a_
china i porsel_a_ni
China i K_i_na
Chinese *(man)* o Kin_e_zos
  (woman) i Kin_e_za
  (adj.) Kin_e_zikos
chocolate i sokol_a_ta
  box of chocolates to koot_i_ me ta
  sokolat_a_kia

chop *(food)* i brizola
  (to cut) kovo
church i eklisia
cigar to pooro
cigarette to tsigaro
city i poli
city center to kendro tis polis
class i THesi
classical music i klasiki moosiki
clean kaTHaros
clear *(obvious)* faneros
  (water) thiavyes
  is that clear? to katalaves?
clever exipnos
clock to roloi
  (alarm) to xipnitiri
close *(near)* konda
  (stuffy) apopniktikos
  (verb) klino
  the store is closed to magazi eklise
clothes ta rooha
club to "club"
  (cards) to bastooni
clutch to debrayaz
coach *(of train)* to vagoni
coat to palto
coathanger i kremastra
cockroach i katsaritha
coffee o kafes
coin to kerma
cold *(adj.)* krios
  (illness) to krioma
collar to kolaro
collection *(stamps, etc.)* i siloyi
color to hroma
color film to enhromo film
comb *(noun)* i tsatsara
  (verb) htenizome
come erhome
  I come from . . . ime apo . . .
  we came last week irThame tin perasmeni evthomatha
  come here! ela!

compartment to vagoni
complicated poliplokos
concert i sinavlia
conditioner *(hair)* to "conditioner"
conductor *(bus)* o ispraktoras
  (orchestra) o maestros
congratulations! sinharitiria!
constipation i thiskiliotis
consulate to proxenio
contact lenses i faki epafis
contraceptive to profilaktiko
cook *(noun)* o mayiras
  (verb) mayirevo
cookie to biskoto
cooking utensils ta mayirika skevi
cool throseros
Corfu i Kerkira
cork o felos
corkscrew to anihtiri
corner i gonia
corridor o thiathromos
cosmetics ta kalindika
cost *(verb)* stihizo
  what does it cost? poso kani afto?
cotton vamvakero
cotton balls to vamvaki
cough *(verb)* viho
  (noun) o vihas
country *(state)* i hora
  (not town) i exohi
cousin *(male)* o exathelfos
  (female) i exathelfi
crab to kavoori
cramp i kramba
crayfish i karavitha
cream i krema
credit card i pistotiki karta
Crete i Kriti
crew to pliroma
crowded yemato kosmo
cruise i krooaziera
crutches i pateritses

cry *(weep)* kleo
   (shout) fonazo
cucumber to agoori
cuff links ta maniketokooba
cup to flitzani
cupboard to doolapi
curlers ta bikooti
curls i bookles
curry metafero
curtain i koortina
customs to Telonio
cut *(noun)* to kopsimo
   (verb) kovo

dad o babas
dairy *(shop)* to galaktopolio
damp igros
dance o horos
dangerous epikinthinos
dark skotinos
daughter i kori
day i imera
dead nekros
deaf koofos
dear *(person)* agapitos
deck chair i politHrona
deep vatHis
deliberately epitithes
dentist o othondiatros
dentures i masela
deny arnoome
   I deny it to arnoome
deodorant to aposmitiko
department store to katastima
departure i anahorisi
develop *(a roll of film)* emfanizo
diamond *(jewel)* to thiamandi
   (cards) to karo
diaper i pana
diarrhea i thiaria
diary to imeroloyio
dictionary to lexiko

die petHeno
diesel to "diesel"
different thiaforetikos
   that's different afto ine alo
   I'd like a different one THelo
   ena alo
difficult thiskolos
dining car to estiatorio too trenoo
dining room i trapezaria
directory *(telephone)* o tilefonikos
   katalogos
dirty vromikos
disabled anapiros
dishwashing liquid to sapooni piaton
distributor *(car)* to distribiooter
dive vooto
diving board i sanitha
divorced horismenos
do kano
dock i prokimea
doctor o yatros
document to engrafo
dog o skilos
doll i kookla
dollar to tholario
door i porta
double room to thiplo thomatio
doughnut to donat
down kato
dress to forema
drink *(verb)* pino
   (noun) to poto
   would you like a drink?
   THelis ena poto?
drinking water to posimo nero
drive *(verb)* othigo
driver o othigos
driver's license to thiploma
   othiyiseos
driving regulations o othikos kothikas
drugstore to farmakio
drunk metHismenos
dry stegnos

dry cleaner to stegnokaTHaristirio
during kata ti thiarkia
dustcloth to xeskonopano
Dutch Olanthikos
duty-free aforoloyita

each (*every*) kaTHenas
  twenty drachma each ikosi thrahmes
  to kaTHena
early noris
earrings ta skoolarikia
ears ta aftia
east i anatoli
easy efkolos
egg to avgo
either: either of them
  opio nane
  either . . . or . . . i . . . i . . .
elastic elastikos
elbow o agonas
electric ilektrikos
electricity to ilektriko
elevator to ansanser
else: something else kati alo
  someone else kapios alos
  somewhere else kapoo aloo
embarrassing dropiastikos
embassy i presvia
embroidery to kendima
emerald to smaragthi
emergency i epigoosa anagi
empty athios
end to telos
engaged (*couple*) aravoniasmenos
  (*occupied*) katilimenos
engine (*car*) i mihani
England i Anglia
English Anglikos
  (*language*) ta Anglika
Englishman o Anglikos
Englishwoman i Anglitha
enlargement i meyenTHisi

enough arketa
entertainment i thiaskethasi
entrance i isothos
envelope o fakelos
eraser i goma
escalator i kinites skales
especially ithi-etera
evening to vrathi
every kaTHe
everyone oli
everything kaTHe ti
everywhere opoothipote
example to parathigma
  for example parathigmatos hari
excellent iperohos
excess baggage to ipervaro
exchange (*verb*) andalaso
exchange rate i timi sinalagmatos
excursion i ekthromi
excuse me? signomi?
  excuse me! signomi!
exit i exothos
expensive akrivos
extension cord i proektasi
eye drops i stagones ya ta
  matia
eyes ta matia

face to prosopo
faint (*unclear*) asafis
  (*verb*) lipoTHimo
  to feel faint esTHanome lipoTHimia
fair (*amusement park*) to paniyiri
  it's not fair then ine thikeo
false teeth ta pseftika thondia
family i ikoyenia
fan (*ventilator*) o anemistiras
  (*enthusiast*) o THavmastis
fan belt to loori too ventilater
far makria
  how far is . . . ? poso makria ine . . . ?
fare i timi too isitirioo

farm to agroktima
farmer o agrotis
fashion i motha
fast grigoros
fat *(of person)* to pahos
  (on meat, etc.) to lipos
father o pateras
feel *(touch)* agizo
  I feel hot zestenome
  I feel like . . . eho epiTHimia ya . . .
  I don't feel well then esTHanome
  kala
feet ta pothia
felt-tip pen o markathoros
ferry to feri-bot
fever o piretos
fiancé o aravoniastikos
fiancée i aravoniastikia
field to horafi
fig to siko
filling *(tooth)* to sfrayisma
  (sandwich, etc.) i yemisi
film to "film"
filter to filtro
finger to thaktilo
fire i fotia
  (blaze) i pirkaya
fire extinguisher o pirosvestiras
firework to pirotehnima
first protos
first aid i protes voiTHies
first name to mikro onoma
fish to psari
fishing to psarema
  to go fishing pao ya psarema
fishing rod to psarokalamo
fish market o psaras
flag i simea
flash *(camera)* to flas
flashlight o fakos
flat *(level)* epipethos
flavor i yefsi
flea o psilos

flight i ptisi
flight attendant *(female)* i aerosinothos
flip-flops i sayionares
flippers ta vatrahopethila
flour to alevri
flower to looloothi
flu i gripi
flute to flaooto
fly *(verb)* peto
  (insect) i miga
fog i omihli
folk music i thimotiki moosiki
food to fai
food poisoning i trofiki
  thilitiriasi
for ya
  for me ya mena
  what for? ya pio logo?
  for a week ya mia evthomatha
foreigner o xenos
forest to thasos
fork to pirooni
fountain pen i pena
fourth tetartos
fracture to katagma
France i Galia
free eleftheros
  (no cost) thore-an
freezer i katapsixi
French Galikos
French fries i tiganites patates
Frenchman o Galos
Frenchwoman i Galitha
friend o filos
friendly filikos
front: in front of . . . brosta apo . . .
frost i pagonia
fruit to frooto
fruit juice o himos frooton
fry tiganizo
frying pan to tigani
full yematos
  I'm full hortasa

full board fool pansi<u>o</u>n
funnel (*for pouring*) to hon<u>i</u>
funny ast<u>i</u>os
  (*odd*) per<u>i</u>-ergos
furniture ta <u>e</u>pipla

garage to gar<u>a</u>z
garbage ta skoop<u>i</u>thia
garbage bag i sak<u>oo</u>la skoopithi<u>o</u>n
garbage can o skoopithondenek<u>e</u>s
garden o k<u>i</u>pos
garlic to sk<u>o</u>rtho
gas i venz<u>i</u>ni
gas-permeable lenses
  i im<u>i</u>skliri fak<u>i</u> epaf<u>i</u>s
gas station to venzin<u>a</u>thiko
gay (*happy*) har<u>oo</u>menos
  (*homosexual*) o om<u>o</u>filofilos
gear i tah<u>i</u>tita
gearshift o mohl<u>o</u>s tahit<u>i</u>ton
German (*man*) o Yerman<u>o</u>s
  (*woman*) i Yerman<u>i</u>tha
  (*adj.*) Yermanik<u>o</u>s
Germany i Yerman<u>i</u>a
get (*fetch*) p<u>e</u>rno
  have you got . . . ? <u>e</u>his . . . ?
  to get the train p<u>e</u>rno to tr<u>e</u>no
  get back: we get back tomorrow
    epistr<u>e</u>foom<u>e</u> <u>a</u>vrio
  to get something back
    p<u>e</u>rno k<u>a</u>ti p<u>i</u>so
get in bes m<u>e</u>sa
  (*arrive*) ft<u>a</u>no
get out vy<u>e</u>no
get up (*rise*) sik<u>o</u>nome
gift to th<u>o</u>ro
gin to "gin"
girl i kop<u>e</u>la
girlfriend i filen<u>a</u>tha
give th<u>i</u>no
glad efharistim<u>e</u>nos
  I'm glad <u>i</u>me eftih<u>i</u>s

glass to yal<u>i</u>
  (*to drink*) to pot<u>i</u>ri
glasses ta yali<u>a</u>
glossy prints i yalister<u>i</u> ekt<u>i</u>posi
gloves ta g<u>a</u>ndia
glue i k<u>o</u>la
goggles i m<u>a</u>ska
gold o hris<u>o</u>s
good kal<u>o</u>s
  good! kal<u>a</u>!
good-bye ya har<u>a</u>
government i kiv<u>e</u>rnisi
granddaughter i egon<u>i</u>
grandfather o pap<u>oo</u>s
grandmother i ya<u>y</u>a
grandson o egon<u>o</u>s
grapes ta staf<u>i</u>lia
grass to grasith<u>i</u>
gray gri
Great Britain i Megali Vretan<u>i</u>a
Greece i El<u>a</u>tha
Greek (*man*) o <u>E</u>linas
  (*woman*) i Elin<u>i</u>tha
  (*adj.*) Elinik<u>o</u>s
  (*language*) ta Elinik<u>a</u>
Greek Orthodox orTH<u>o</u>thoxos
green pr<u>a</u>sinos
grill i psistari<u>a</u>
grocery store to bak<u>a</u>liko
ground cloth o moosam<u>a</u>s
ground floor to is<u>o</u>yio
guarantee (*noun*) i egi-<u>i</u>si
  (*verb*) egio<u>o</u>me
guard o f<u>i</u>lakas
guidebook o othig<u>o</u>s
guitar i kiT<u>H</u>ara
gun (*rifle*) to <u>o</u>plo
  (*pistol*) to pist<u>o</u>li

hair ta mali<u>a</u>
haircut (*for man*) to k<u>oo</u>rema
  (*for woman*) to k<u>o</u>psimo
hairdresser i komotr<u>i</u>a

hair dryer to pistolaki
hair spray i lak
half miso
  half an hour misi ora
half board i demi pansion
ham to zabon
hamburger to hamboorger
hammer to sfiri
hand to heri
handbag i tsanda
hand brake to hirofreno
handkerchief to hartomandilo
handle *(door)* to herooli
handsome oreos
hangover o ponokefalos
happy eftihismenos
hard skliros
  (difficult) thiskolos
hard lenses i skliri faki epafis
hardware store o sitheras
hat to kapelo
have eho
  I don't have . . . then eho . . .
  can I have . . . ? boro na eho . . . ?
  have you got . . . ? ehete . . . ?
  I have to go now prepi na
    piyeno tora
hay fever o piretos ek hortoo
he aftos
head to kefali
headache o ponokefalos
headlights i provolis
hear akoo-o
hearing aid ta akoostika
heart i karthia
heart attack i karthiaki prosvoli
heating i THermansi
heavy varis
heel to takooni
hello ya soo
help *(noun)* i voiTHia
  (verb) voiTHo
  help! voiTHia!

her: it's for her ine ya ftin
  give it to her thostis to
  her book to vivlio tis
  her house to spiti tis
  her shoes ta papootsia tis
  it's hers ine thiko tis
high psilos
highway i eTHniki othos
hill o lofos
him: it's for him ine ya fton
  give it to him thostoo to
his: his book to vivlio too
  his house to spiti too
  his shoes ta papootsia too
  it's his ine thiko too
history i istoria
hitchhike kano oto-stop
hobby to "hobby"
Holland i Olanthia
holiday i thiakopes
honest timios
honey to meli
honeymoon o minas too melitos
hood *(car)* to kapo
horn *(car)* to klaxon
  (animal) to kerato
horrible fovero
hospital to nosokomio
hot water bottle i THermofora
hour i ora
house to spiti
how? pos?
hungry: I'm hungry pinao
hurry: I'm in a hurry viazome
husband o sizigos

I ego
ice o pagos
ice cream to pagoto
ice cube to pagaki
if ean
ignition i miza

ill arostos
immediately amesos
impossible athinato
in mesa
India i Inthia
Indian *(man)* o Inthos
  (woman) i Inthi
  (adj.) Inthikos
indigestion i thispepsia
inexpensive ftinos
infection i molinsi
information i plirofories
injection i enesi
injury to atihima
ink to melani
inner tube i sabrela
insect to endomo
insect repellent o apoтнitis edomon
insomnia i aipnia
insurance i asfalia
interesting enthiaferon
interpret thierminevo
invitation i prosklisi
Ireland i Irlanthia
Irish Irlanthikos
Irishman o Irlanthos
Irishwoman i Irlantheza
iron *(metal, for clothes)* to sithero
is: he/she/it is . . . ine . . .
island to nisi
it afto
itch *(noun)* i fagoora
  it itches me troi

jacket to sakaki
jacuzzi to "jacuzzi"
jam i marmelatha
jazz i "jazz"
jealous ziliaris
jeans to "jean"
jellyfish i tsoohtra
jeweler to kosmimatopolio

job i thoolia
jog *(verb)* kano "jogging"
  to go for a jog pao ya "jogging"
jogging suit i aтнlitiki forma
joke to astio
journey to taxithi
just: it's just arrived molis
  eftase
  I've just one left eho mono ena

key to klithi
kidney to nefro
kilo to kilo
kilometer to hiliometro
kitchen i koozina
knee to gonato
knife to maheri
knit pleko
knitting needle i velona pleximatos
know: I don't know then xero

label i etiketa
lace i thantela
laces *(of shoe)* ta korthonia
lake i limni
lamb to arni
lamp i laba
lampshade to labater
land *(noun)* i yi
  (verb) prosyionome
language i glosa
large megalos
last *(final)* telefteos
  last week i perasmeni evthomatha
  last month o perasmenos minas
  at last! epi teloos!
last name to epiтнeto
late: it's getting late vrathiazi
  the bus is late leoforio aryise
laugh to yelio
laundromat to plindirio roohon

laundry *(place)* to katHaristirio
   (dirty clothes) ta aplita
laundry detergent to aporipandiko
laxative to katHartiko
lazy tebelis
leaf to filo
leaflet to thiafimistiko
learn matHeno
leather to therma
left *(not right)* aristera
   there's nothing left
   then emine tipota
leftovers ta apominaria
leg to pothi
lemon to lemoni
lemonade i lemonatha
length to mikos
lens o fakos
less ligotera
lesson to matHima
letter to grama
lettuce to marooli
library i vivliotHiki
license i athia
license plate i pinakitha
life i zoi
lift: could you give me a lift?
   borite na me pate?
light *(not heavy)* elafris
   (not dark) apalos
lighter o anaptiras
lighter fuel ta aerio anaptira
light meter to fotometro
like: I like you moo aresis
   I like swimming moo aresi to
   kolibi
   it's like . . . miazi me . . .
lime *(fruit)* to kitro
line *(of people)* i oora
line up *(verb)* beno stin oora
lip balm to vootiro kakao
lipstick to krayion
liqueur to liker

list i lista
liter to litro
litter ta skoopithia
little *(small)* mikros
   it's a little big ine ligo megalo
   just a little ligaki
liver to sikoti
lobster o astakos
lollipop to glifitzoori
long makris
   how long does it take? posi ora kani?
lost and found i hamenes aposkeves
lot: a lot pola
loud thinatos
   (color) htipitos
lounge to saloni
love *(noun)* i agapi
   (verb) agapo
lover *(man)* o erastis
   (woman) i eromeni
low hamilos
luck i tihi
   good luck! kali tihi!
lunch to yevma

magazine to periothiko
mail ta gramata
mailbox to gramatokivotio
mailman o tahithromos
make kano
make up to "make up"
man o andras
manager o thiefтнindis
map o hartis
   a map of Athens enas hartis tis
   АтНines
marble to marmaro
margarine i margarini
market i agora
marmalade i marmelatha
married pandremenos
mascara i maskara

mass *(church)* i litoorgia
mast to katarti
match *(light)* to spirto
  (sports) to "match"
material *(cloth)* to ifasma
mattress to stroma
maybe isos
me: it's for me ine ya mena
  give it to me thosto moo
meal to yevma
meat to kreas
mechanic o mihanikos
medicine to farmako
meeting i sinandisis
melon to peponi
menu to menoo
message to minima
middle: in the middle sti mesi
midnight ta mesanihta
milk to gala
mine: it's mine ine thiko moo
mineral water to emfialomeno nero
minute to lepto
mirror o kaтнreftis
mistake to laтнos
  to make a mistake kano laтнos
mom i mama
monastery to monastiri
money ta lefta
month o minas
monument to mnimio
moon to fegari
moped to mihanaki me petalia
more perisoteros
  more or less pano-kato
morning to proi
  in the morning to proi
mosaic to psifithoto
mosquito to koonoopi
mother i mitera
motorboat varka me mihani
motorcycle to mihanaki
mountain to voono

mouse to pondiki
moustache to moostaki
mouth to stoma
move metakino
  don't move! mi kooniese!
  (house) metakomizo
movie to ergo
movie theater o kinimatografos
Mr. kirios
Mrs. kiria
much: not much ohi poli
mug i koopa
  a mug of coffee ena flitzani kafe
mule to moolari
museum to moosio
mushroom to manitari
music i moosiki
musical instrument to moosiko
  organo
musician o moosikos
mussels ta mithia
mustard i moostartha
my: my book to vivlio moo
  my bag i tsanda moo
  my keys ta klithia moo
mythology i miтноloyia

nail *(metal)* to karfi
  (finger) to nihi
nail file i lima nihion
nail polish to mano
name to onoma
napkin i hartopetseta
narrow stenos
near: near the door konda sti porta
  near Chicago konda sto sikago
necessary aparetitos
necklace to kolie
need *(verb)* hriazome
  I need . . . hriazome . . .
  there's no need then hriazete
needle i velona

negative *(photo)* to arnitiko
neither: neither of them kanenas
  apo aftoos
  neither . . . nor . . . oote . . . oote . . .
nephew o anipsios
never pote
new kenooryios
news ta nea
newsagent to praktorio
  efimerithon
newsstand i efimeritha
New Zealand i Nea Zilanthia
New Zealander
  (man) o Neozilanthos
  (woman) i Neozilantheza
next epomenos
  next week i epomeni
  evthomatha
  next month o epomenos minas
  what next? ti alo?
nice oreos
niece i anipsia
night i nihta
nightclub to nihterino kendro
nightgown to nihtiko
no *(response)* ohi
  I have no money then eho lefta
noisy THorivothis
noon to mesimeri
north o voras
Northern Ireland i Voria Irlanthia
nose i miti
not then
notebook to blokaki
nothing tipota
novel to miTHistorima
now tora
nowhere pooTHena
nudist o yimnistis
number o ariTHmos
nurse i nosokoma
nut *(fruit)* i xiri karpi
  (for bolt) to paximathi

occasionally pote-pote
octopus to htapothi
of too
office to grafio
often sihna
oil to lathi
ointment i alifi
OK endaxi
old palios
olive i elia
omelette i omeleta
on pano
one enas, mia, ena
onion to kremithi
only mono
open *(verb)* anigo
  (adj.) anihtos
opposite: opposite the hotel
  apenandi apo to xenothohio
optician o optikos
or i
orange *(color)* portokali
  (fruit) to portokali
orange juice i portokalatha
orchestra i orhistra
ordinary *(normal)* kanonikos
organ to organo
  (music) to armonio
our thikos mas
  it's ours ine thiko mas
out: he's out ine exo
outside exo
over pano apo
  over there eki pera
oyster to strithi

pacifier i pipila
pack of cards i trapoola
package to paketo
  (parcel) to thema
packet to paketo
  a packet of . . . ena paketo . . .

padlock to look<u>e</u>to
page i sel<u>i</u>tha
pain o p<u>o</u>nos
paint (noun) to hr<u>o</u>ma
pair to zevg<u>a</u>ri
pajamas i pitz<u>a</u>mes
Pakistan to Pakist<u>a</u>n
Pakistani (man) o Pakistan<u>o</u>s
   (woman) i Pakistan<u>i</u>
   (adj.) Pakistanik<u>o</u>s
pale hlom<u>o</u>s
pancakes i th<u>i</u>ples
pants to pandel<u>o</u>ni
paper to hart<u>i</u>
parents i gon<u>i</u>s
park (noun) to p<u>a</u>rko
   (verb) park<u>a</u>ro
parking lights ta f<u>o</u>ta por<u>i</u>as
parsley o maindan<u>o</u>s
party (celebration) to p<u>a</u>rti
   (group) to groop
   (political) to k<u>o</u>ma
pass (in car) prospern<u>o</u>
passenger epiv<u>a</u>tis
passport to thiavat<u>i</u>rio
pasta ta zimarik<u>a</u>
pastry shop to zaharoplast<u>i</u>o
path to monop<u>a</u>ti
pay plir<u>o</u>no
peach to roth<u>a</u>kino
peanuts ta fist<u>i</u>kia
pear to ahl<u>a</u>thi
pearl to margarit<u>a</u>ri
peas ta biz<u>e</u>lia
pedestrian o pez<u>o</u>s
peg (clothes) i krem<u>a</u>stra
pen to stil<u>o</u>
pencil to mol<u>i</u>vi
pencil sharpener i x<u>i</u>stra
peninsula i hers<u>o</u>nisos
penknife o sooy<u>a</u>s
pen pal o f<u>i</u>los thi' alilograf<u>i</u>as
people i anTHr<u>o</u>pi

pepper (& salt) to pip<u>e</u>ri
   (red/green) i piperi<u>a</u>
peppermints i m<u>e</u>ndes
per: per night tin vrath<u>i</u>a
perfect t<u>e</u>lios
perfume to <u>a</u>roma
perhaps <u>i</u>sos
perm i perman<u>a</u>nt
petticoat to kombinez<u>o</u>n
photograph (noun) i fotograf<u>i</u>a
   (verb) fotograf<u>i</u>zo
photographer o fot<u>o</u>grafos
phrase book to vivl<u>i</u>o x<u>e</u>non thial<u>o</u>gon
piano to pi<u>a</u>no
pickpocket o portof<u>o</u>las
picnic to "picnic"
pillow to maxil<u>a</u>ri
pilot o pil<u>o</u>tos
pin i karf<u>i</u>tsa
pine (tree) to p<u>e</u>fko
pineapple o anan<u>a</u>s
pink roz
pipe (for smoking) to tsib<u>oo</u>ki
   (for water) i sol<u>i</u>na
piston to pist<u>o</u>ni
pizza i p<u>i</u>zza
place to m<u>e</u>ros
plant to fit<u>o</u>
plastic to plastik<u>o</u>
plastic bag i plastik<u>i</u> sak<u>oo</u>la
plate to pi<u>a</u>to
platform i platf<u>o</u>rma
play (theater) to THeatrik<u>o</u>
   <u>e</u>rgo
please parakal<u>o</u>
plug (electrical) i br<u>i</u>sa
   (sink) to v<u>oo</u>loma
pocket to ts<u>e</u>pi
poison to thilit<u>i</u>rio
police i astinom<u>i</u>a
police officer o astinomik<u>o</u>s
police station to astinomik<u>o</u> tm<u>i</u>ma
politics ta politik<u>a</u>

poor ftohos
 (*bad quality*) kakos
pop music i pop moosiki
pork to hirino
port to limani
porter (*for luggage*) o ah-THoforos
 (*hotel*) o THiroros
possible thinaton
post (*noun*) ta gramata
 (*verb*) tahithromo
postcard i kart-postal
poster to poster
post office to tahithromio
potato i patata
potato chips ta tsips
poultry ta poolerika
pound (*weight*) i libra
powder i skoni
prawn i garitha
 (*bigger*) i karavitha
prescription i sindayi
pretty (*beautiful*) omorfos
 (*quite*) arketa
priest o papas
private ithiotikos
problem to provlima
 what's the problem? ti simveni?
public to kino
pull travo
puncture to kendima
purple porfiro
purse to portofoli
push sprohno

quality i piotita
question i erotisi
quick grigoros
quiet isihos
quite (*fairly*) arketa
 (*fully*) teljos

radiator to psiyio
radio to rathiofono
radish to rapanaki
railroad line i grames too trenoo
rain i vrohi
rain boots i galotses
raincoat to athiavroho
raisins i stafithes
rare (*uncommon*) spanios
 (*steak*) misopsimenos
rat o arooreos
razor blades ta xirafakia
read thiavazo
reading lamp to fos too grafioo
 (*bed*) to potatif
ready etimos
receipt i apothixi
receptionist o reseptionistas
record (*music*) o thiskos
 (*sports, etc.*) to rekor
record player to pik-ap
record store to thiskopolio
red kokino
refreshments ta anapsiktika
refrigerator to psiyio
registered letter to sistimeno
 grama
relative o sigenis
relax iremo
religion i THriskia
remember THimame
 I don't remember then THimame
rent (*verb*) nikiazo
reservation to klisimo THesis
reservation office to praktorio isitirion
rest (*remainder*) to ipolipo
 (*relax*) xekoorazome
restaurant to estiatorio
restaurant car to estiatorio trenoo
restroom (*men's*) i tooaleta anthron
 (*women's*) i tooaleta yinekon
return epistrefo
Rhodes i Rothos

rice to rizi
rich ploosios
right (correct) sostos
  (direction) thexia
ring (wedding, etc.) to thahtilithi
ripe orimos
river to potami
road o thromos
rock (stone) o vrahos
  (music) i moosiki rok
roll (bread) to psomaki
  (verb) kilo
roller skates ta patinia
roof i orofi
  (flat) i taratsa
room to thomatio
  (space) to meros
rope to s-hini
rose to triandafilo
round (circular) strogilos
  it's my round ine i sira moo
rowboat i varka me koopia
rubber to lastiho
rubber band to lastihaki
ruby (stone) to roobini
rug (mat) to halaki
ruins ta eripia
ruler o harakas
rum to roomi
run (verb: person) treho
runway o thiathromos

sad lipimenos
safe asfalis
safety pin i paramana
sailboat to istioforo
salad i salata
salami to salami
sale (at reduced prices) i ekptosis
salmon o solomos
salt to alati

same: the same dress to ithio forema
  the same people i ithi-i anthropi
  same again, please ena akoma
sand i amos
sandals ta sandalia
sand dunes i amolofi
sandwich to "sandwich"
sanitary napkins i servietes
sauce i saltsa
saucepan i katsarola
sauna i sa-oona
sausage to lookaniko
say lego
  what did you say? ti ipes?
  how do you say . . . ? pos THa
  poome . . . ?
scarf to kaskol
  (head) to mandili
school to s-holio
scissors to psalithi
Scotland i Skotia
Scottish Skotsezikos
screw i vitha
screwdriver to katsavithi
sea i THalasa
seafood ta THalasina
seat i THesi
seat belt i zoni asfalias
second thefteros
second floor to proto patoma
see kitazo
  I can't see then vlepo
  I see katalava
sell poolo
separate xehoristos
separated horismenos
serious sovaros
several arketi
sew ravo
shampoo to sambooan
shave (noun) to xirisma
  (verb) xirizome
shaving cream o afros xirismatos

shawl to sali

she afti

sheet to sendoni

shell to ostrako

sherry to seri

ship to karavi

shirt to pookamiso

shoelaces ta korthonia

shoe polish to verniki papootsion

shoes ta papootsia

shoe store to katastima ipothimaton

shop to magazi

shopping ta psonia

  to go shopping pao ya psonia

short kondos

shorts to "shorts"

shoulder o omos

shower (*bath*) to doos

  (*rain*) i bora

shrimp i garitha

shutter (*camera*) to thiafragma

  (*window*) i pantzoori

sick (*ill*) arostos

  I feel sick ime athiaтнetos

side (*edge*) plevra

  I'm on her side ime me to meros tis

sidewalk to pezothromio

sights: the sights of . . .

  ta axioтнeata tis . . .

silk to metaxoto

silver (*color*) asimi

  (*metal*) to asimi

simple aplos

sing tragootho

single (*one*) monos

  (*unmarried*) anipandros

single room to mono thomatio

sink o niptiras

sister i athelfi

skid (*verb*) glistrao

skin cleanser to galaktoma kaтнarismoo

skirt i foosta

sky o ooranos

sleep (*noun*) o ipnos

  (*verb*) kimame

  to go to sleep pao ya ipno

sleeping bag to "sleeping bag"

sleeping pill to ipnotiko hapi

slippers i pandofles

slow argos

small mikros

smell (*noun*) i mirothia

  (*verb*) mirizo

smile (*noun*) to hamoyelo

  (*verb*) hamoyelo

smoke (*noun*) o kapnos

  (*verb*) kapnizo

snack to prohino yevma

snorkel o anapnefstiras

snow to hioni

so: so good poli kala

  not so much ohi toso poli

soaking solution (*for contact lenses*) igro sindirisis fakon epafis

soccer to pothosfero

soccer ball i bala

socks i kaltses

soda water i sotha

soft lenses i malaki faki epafis

somebody kapios

somehow kapos

something kati

sometimes merikes fores

somewhere kapoo

son o yios

song to tragoothi

sorry! pardon!

  I'm sorry signomi

soup i soopa

south o notos

South Africa i Notios Afriki

South African

  (*man*) o Notioafrikanos

  (*woman*) i Notioafrikana

  (*adj.*) Notioafrikanikos

souvenir to enTHimio
spade *(shovel)* to ftiari
  (cards) to bastooni
Spain i Ispania
Spanish *(adj.)* Ispanikos
spare parts ta andalaktika
spark plug to boozi
speak milao
  do you speak . . . ? milate . . . ?
  I don't speak . . . then milo . . .
speed i tahitita
speed limit to orio tahititos
speedometer to konter
spider i arahni
spinach to spanaki
spoon to kootali
sprain to strabooligma
spring *(mechanical)* to elatirio
  (season) i anixi
stadium to stathio
staircase i skala
stairs ta skalopatia
stamp to gramatosimo
stapler o sinthetiras
star to asteri
  (movie) i star
start i arhi
  (verb) arhizo
station o staTHmos
statue to agalma
steak i brizola
steal klevo
  it's been stolen to klepsane
steering wheel to timoni
sting *(noun)* to tsooximo
  (verb) tsoozo
  it stings tsoozi
stockings i kaltses
stomach to stomahi
stomachache o stomahoponos
stop *(verb)* stamato
  (bus stop) i stasi
  stop! stamata!

storm i THiela
strawberry i fraoola
stream *(small river)* to potamaki
street o thromos
string *(cord)* o spagos
  (guitar, etc.) i horthi
stroller to karotsaki
student o maTHitis
stupid vlakas
suburbs ta proastia
sugar i zahari
suit *(noun)* to koostoomi
  (verb) teriazo
  it suits you soo pai
suitcase i valitsa
sun o ilios
sunbathe kano ilioTHerapia
sunburn to kapsimo apo ton ilio
sunglasses ta yalia ilioo
sunny: it's sunny ehi liakatha
suntan to mavrisma
suntan lotion to andiliako
supermarket to "supermarket"
supplement epipleon
sweat *(noun)* o ithrotas
  (verb) ithrono
sweater to poolover
sweatshirt i fanela
sweet glikos
swimming pool i pisina
swimming trunks to mayio
Swiss *(man)* o Elvetos
  (woman) i Elvetitha
  (adj.) Elvetikos
switch o thiakoptis
Switzerland i Elvetia
synagogue i sinagoyi

table to trapezi
tablet to thiskio
taillights ta piso fota
take perno

takeoff *(noun)* i apoyiosi
take off *(verb)* apoyionome
take-out *(food)* ya to thromo
talcum powder to talk
talk *(noun)* i sizitisi
    (verb) milo
tall psilos
tampon to "Tampax"®
tangerine to mandarini
tap i vrisi
tape *(adhesive, invisible)* to "sellotape"®
tapestry i tapetsaria
tea to tsai
telegram to tilegrafima
telephone *(noun)* to tilefono
    (verb) tilefono
telephone booth o tilefonikos THalamos
telephone call to tilefonima
television i tileorasi
temperature i THermokrasia
tent i skini
tent peg o pasalos skinis
tent pole o stilos skinis
thank *(verb)* efharisto
    thanks efharisto
    thank you sas efharisto
that: that bus ekino to leoforio
    that man ekinos o andras
    that woman ekini i yineka
    what's that? ti ine ekino?
    I think that . . . nomizo oti . . .
their: their room to thomatio toos
    their books ta vivlia toos
    it's theirs ine thiko toos
them: it's for them ine yaftoos
    give it to them thosto toos
then tote
there eki
these: these things afta ta pragmata
    these are mine afta ine thika moo
they afti
thick pahis

thin leptos
think nomizo/skeftome
    I think so etsi nomizo
    I'll think about it THa to skefto
thirsty: I'm thirsty thipso
this: this bus afto to leoforio
    this man aftos o andras
    this woman afti i yineka
    what's this? ti ine afto?
    this is Mr. . . . apotho o kirios . . .
those: those things afta ta pragmata
    those are his afta ine thika too
throat o lemos
throat pastilles i pastilies lemoo
thumbtack i pineza
thunderstorm i kateyitha
ticket to isitirio
tie *(noun)* i gravata
    (verb) theno
time i ora
    what's the time? ti ora ine?
timetable to programa
tip *(money)* to poorbooar
    (end) miti
tire to lastiho
tired koorasmenos
    I feel tired ime koorasmenos
tissues ta hartomandila
to: to the US stin Ameriki
    to the station sto staTHmo
    to the doctor sto yatro
toast to tost
tobacco o kapnos
toilet i tooaleta
toilet paper to harti iyias
tomato i domata
tomorrow avrio
tongue i glosa
tonic to "tonic"
tonight apopse
too *(also)* episis
    (excessive) para poli
toothache o ponothondos

toothbrush i othond_o_voortsa
toothpaste i othond_o_krema
tour i peri-iyisi
tourist o toorist_a_s
towel i pets_e_ta
tower o p_i_rgos
town i p_o_li
town hall to thimarh_i_o
toy to pehn_i_thi
toy shop to kat_a_stima pehnithi_o_n
tractor to trakt_e_r
tradition i par_a_thosi
traffic i k_i_nisi
traffic lights ta fan_a_ria
trailer to rimoolk_o_
train to tr_e_no
translate metafr_a_zo
transmission _(for car)_ i met_a_thosi kin_i_seos
travel agency to taxithiotik_o_ graf_i_o
traveler's check i taxithiotik_i_ epitay_i_
tray o th_i_skos
tree to th_e_ndro
truck to fortig_o_
trunk _(car)_ to port-bag_a_z
try prosp_a_tho
tunnel i s_i_raga
Turk _(man)_ o T_o_orkos
  (woman) i T_o_ork_a_la
Turkey i Toork_i_a
Turkish T_o_orkikos
turn signal o th_i_ktis
tweezers to tsibith_a_ki
typewriter i grafomihan_i_

umbrella i obr_e_la
uncle o TH_i_os
under k_a_to
underground o ip_o_yios
underpants to s_o_vrako

undershirt to fanel_a_ki
university to panepist_i_mio
unmarried an_i_pandros
until m_e_hri
unusual asin_i_THistos
up p_a_no
  (upward) pros ta p_a_no
urgent ep_i_gon
us: it's for us _i_ne ya mas
  give it to us th_o_sto mas
use _(noun)_ i hrisim_o_tis
  (verb) hrisimopi_o_
  it's no use then ax_i_zi ton k_o_po
useful hr_i_simos
usual sin_i_THism_e_nos
usually sin_i_THos

vacancy _(room)_ ken_o_s
vacuum cleaner i ilektrik_i_ sk_oo_pa
valley i kil_a_tha
valve i valv_i_tha
vanilla i van_i_lia
vase to v_a_zo
veal to mos-har_a_ki
vegetables ta lahanik_a_
vegetarian _(person)_ o hortof_a_gos
vehicle to trohof_o_ro
very pol_i_
view i TH_e_a
viewfinder to sk_o_peftro
villa i "villa"
village to hori_o_
vinegar to x_i_thi
violin to viol_i_
visa i v_i_za
visit _(noun)_ i ep_i_skepsi
  (verb) episk_e_ptome
visitor o episk_e_ptis
vitamin tablet i vitam_i_ni
vodka i v_o_dka
voice i fon_i_

waiter o servitoros
waiter! garson!
waiting room to saloni
waitress i garsona
Wales i Ooalia
walk *(noun)* to perpatima
  (verb) perpato
  to go for a walk pao volta
wall o tihos
wallet to portofoli
war o polemos
wardrobe i doolapa
warm zestos
was: I was imoon
  he was itan
  she was itan
  it was itan
wasp i sfiga
watch *(noun)* to roloi
  (verb) parakolooтно
water to nero
waterfall o katarahtis
wave *(noun)* to kima
  (verb) hereto
we emis
weather o keros
wedding o gamos
week i evthomatha
Welsh Ooalikos
were: we were imastan
  you were isastan
  (sing. familiar) isoon
  they were itan
west thitikos
wet vregmenos
what? ti?
wheel i rotha
wheelchair i anapiriki polithrona
when? pote?
where? poo?

whether kata poso
which? pios?
whiskey to "whiskey"
white aspros
who? pios?
why? yati?
wide platis
wife i sizigos
wind o anemos
windbreaker *(jacket)* to athiavroho
window to paraтнiro
windshield to parbriz
windshield wiper o ialokaтнaristiras
wine to krasi
wine list o katalogos krasion
wing to ftero
with me
without horis
wood to xilo
wool to mali
word i lexi
work *(noun)* i thoolia
  (verb) thoolevo
worry beads to kobolo-i
wrench to klithi
wrapping paper harti peritiligmatos
  (for presents) harti ya thora
wrist o karpos
writing paper to harti alilografias
wrong laтнos

year o hronos
yellow kitrinos
yes ne
yesterday htes
yet akoma
  not yet ohi akoma
yogurt to yaoorti
you esis
  (sing. familiar) esi

your: your book
   (familiar) to vivl<u>i</u>o soo
   (polite) to vivl<u>i</u>o sas
   your shoes
   (familiar) ta papootsi<u>a</u> soo
   (polite) ta papootsi<u>a</u> sas
yours: is it yours?
   (familiar) <u>i</u>ne thik<u>o</u> soo?
   (polite) <u>i</u>ne thik<u>o</u> sas?
youth hostel o xen<u>o</u>nas n<u>e</u>on

zipper to fermoo<u>a</u>r
zoo o zo-oloyik<u>o</u>s k<u>i</u>pos